It's All About the People

Author Gary W. McConnell

and Mason Canyon

Published by Espy Publishing Company Summerville, GA

I

Copyright©2019 by Gary W. McConnell

All rights reserved. No part of this book may be reproduced or used in any manner without written permission of the copyright owner except for the use of quotations in a book review.

First edition February 2019
Second printing April 2019
Third printing May 2019

ISBN-13: 978-1-7336055-0-2

Published by Espy Publishing Company

Dedication

This book is dedicated with love and affection to my wife, Diane; my daughter, Rebecca; my granddaughter, McKenna (Mac); and the wonderful people of Chattooga County!

Foreword

I have had the distinct pleasure of knowing Gary McConnell as a close personal friend for his entire lifetime, and as well his father and mother. Gary's father was John Frank McConnell, a much loved and respected farmer, community leader and Chattooga County Sheriff until his untimely and tragic death. Marguerite, his mother, was known to all as a magnetic person who could charm a snake, who possessed a high degree of intelligence, charisma and a demanding sense of presence. It was from this background that helped mold the character and leadership qualities of Gary. He could not have had better role models.

Within a few days after Sheriff McConnell's death, Gary was appointed to serve the remainder of his dad's term – a great challenge as well as a remarkable opportunity for a young man of 22 years, who by virtue of his father's tragic death had suddenly become the youngest Sheriff in the history of Georgia.

Gary rose to the occasion and by hard work, patience and resolve and with his vision and leadership the Chattooga County Sheriff's office became one of the best law enforcement units in Northwest Georgia. His law enforcement duties were exercised with a "light touch" but with a firm understanding of fairness and respect for constitutional rights. By his fellow Chattooga Countians he was rewarded by a return to office – term after term where he served as Sheriff from

1967 to 1976 and then again from 1981-1991. His time as Sheriff could be symbolized by these words "Do your duty in all things, you cannot do more. You should never wish to do less."

After his long tenure in law enforcement had ended he returned with a determined vigor to serve his State when Governor Zell Miller appointed him as the Director of GEMA, where he served for 8 years.

As Director of GEMA, he worked tirelessly in assisting counties and fellow Georgians who had suffered natural disasters by storms, floods and other plagues. It was a difficult but rewarding position where by his dedication and skillful understanding, he rendered vital assistance to the injured and needy where properties and people had been either injured or destroyed by natural disasters. During this period, he devoted countless hours in employing state aid to assist others and managing the logistical knowhow in getting the aid to the proper source. On more than one occasion, I heard Governor Miller say, "Gary McConnell has made a great contribution to the State. I could not have appointed anyone who would have had a better understanding of what to do and how to do it."

After 8 years with Governor Miller and during the administration of Governor Barnes, he was again appointed director of GEMA for another 4 years, where he continued with the same resolve and dedication. As it was with Governor Miller, it was equally so with Governor Barnes who praised his continuing efforts with a stream of accolades.

After several years of working with private industry he has returned home where he resides with his devoted wife, Diane, who in all of his endeavors, accomplishments, trials and transitions, has been one of his most accomplished ardent supporters and admirers.

Gary McConnell is a person who in all of his public offices and appointments, has served his State and Nation with great distinction and who has made meaningful and worthy contributions that are highly significant to the public good.

As the poet once opined, Gary has miles to walk, to walk before he sleeps. The future may yet yield a call to duty for other accomplishments.

Bobby Lee Cook Sr.

Nationally Recognized Attorney

Summerville, Georgia

Acknowledgments

There are far too many people to acknowledge by individual name that have made this book possible in one way or another. However, there are a few people that I would like to say a special thanks to for their assistance in making this book a reality.

* Ken Anderson
* Angela McBride Amos
* Roy E. Barnes
* Johnny Bass
* Chattanooga Times-Free Press
* Chattooga County School System
* Tommy & Sandra Cobb
* Bobby Lee Cook Sr.
* Lann Cordle
* Gene Espy
* Greg Espy
* Cindy Hall
* Don Henderson
* Max Hollis
* The Late Zell Miller
* J. Terry Norris
* The Late Emmett Nunn
* Pamela Purcell
* Rome News-Tribune
* Trina Hembree Sheets
* The Summerville News
* Lee Sweat
* Tommy Toles
* Trion City School System
* U.S. National Archives & Records Administration
* Kenneth C. Zirkel

Introduction

There is an old African proverb which states that "It takes a village to raise a child."

This fact was so true, when at 22, I lost my best friend, my Father and the sheriff, when my Father died at age 53.

The wonderful people of Chattooga County opened their hearts and minds when I needed it the most. This support enabled me to mature and try to live up to the expectations that they had placed on me to be of service to others, especially those not as fortunate as me, for the rest of my life.

CONTENTS

1
The Beginning

A deep-rooted desire to help others steered my dad onto a path that not only changed his life, but also put me on a similar road. His moral compass has guided me as I've strived to follow in his footsteps and beyond.

John Frank and Marguerite McConnell

It's All About The People

Little did I know that my dad's commitment to create a safer community would lead me on a journey where I would meet not one but five Presidents of the United States. That journey would also have me traveling around the U.S. and abroad to help prepare others to deal with safety issues on a major scale.

None of the following stories would have been possible without tremendous family, community, friends, and employees support. This was not a one-person journey and could not have been accomplished without the commitment, leadership, and support from so many amazing people throughout the years of my career.

My roots, the McConnell roots, are buried deep in Chattooga County (GA) soil. My dad's family started farming in Chattooga in the early 1800s. Their land came from early land grants the government sold to settlers after the Indians were removed from the area during the Trail of Tears.

My mother's family was originally from Walker County. She graduated from Jefferson Davis High School in Vicksburg, MS in 1932. She returned to NW Georgia where she was born, to work in the glove mill for Riegel Textiles during the depression. She met and married my dad and they settled down in Chattooga County.

My parents were carrying on the tradition of farming in the Teloga Community in 1960 when my dad was approached by a group of community

2

Gary W. McConnell

Chattooga jail key circa 1960-1985

leaders. They wanted him to run for the Office of Sheriff. The county was overrun with bootleggers, moonshiners, and gambling. It seemed nothing was being done to stop them and the leaders wanted a change. Chattooga was a dry county, meaning alcohol sales of any kind were unlawful. Regardless of that law, alcohol was available throughout the county in abundance and little was being done to control it.

After giving it some thought and with the support of my mother, my dad decided to give it a go. He ran against the incumbent Sheriff Fred Stewart. It was a bitter race and despite my dad's hard work, Stewart was reelected.

The election was not the only loss of the day. The county and much of the state of Georgia was hit hard with a record ice storm that was already causing problems by the time the polls closed that evening. The storm's effects lasted for several weeks with roads closed and power outages. We lost some 600 head of cattle causing further financial hardship after a losing campaign.

Chattooga's sole county commissioner at the time, John Jones, asked my dad to take on the job as Warden of the county work camp. The work camp was where convicted prisoners were housed locally. They were responsible for doing maintenance work on the county's roads and other county properties.

Dad oversaw the operation until 1964 when

he was approached again by community leaders about running for sheriff. Nothing had improved in the county. The problems with moonshiners and bootleggers (people who sold alcohol illegally in our dry county) were still ongoing. He decided to run again. His campaign promise was to rid the county of these problems.

Prior to this, Dad had suffered a stroke on May 12, 1963. He had only partial use of his right arm. The summer before the '64 election I came home from college to help him campaign. When he was elected, I decided not to return to my studies at college to be a veterinarian but to stay home and work for him -- sort of be his right-hand man so to speak.

2
Chattooga County Sheriff John Frank McConnell

Dad took office on January 1, 1965, just as the state decided to change the way it paid sheriffs. The prior administration had been paid on a fee system where they were paid solely by the fees they collected. From those fees, the sheriff had to pay his deputies, provide his own transportation, and feed and

Sheriff John Frank McConnell

care for the prisoners. Dad was paid a straight salary - $750 a month - and the county had to provide the transportation, deputies' salaries, as well as take care of the prisoners.

When we went into office, the newly elected

6

Deputy Gary McConnell (left) and his father, Sheriff John Frank McConnell, are shown with one of the two new patrol cars the sheriff's department received a month after Sheriff McConnell took office in 1965.

county commissioner, Harry Powell, gave us two rental cars, four badges, four .38 caliber Smith and Wesson handguns, and one radio. There were no radios in the cars and it was a couple of months before we got any.

There were four of us - Dad, me, Randy Roberts (who was chief deputy), and Bert Tucker. Barney Sanders was the jailer. There were seven inmates in the jail at the time and the sheriff's living quarters were adjacent to the jail.

During those early years of our administration,

the jail closed at 10 o'clock at night. There was an intercom between the inmates in the cell block and the living quarters so if a prisoner needed something they could buzz the house. If calls came in from midnight until 7 o'clock the next morning, my mother would answer in the living quarters and dispatch a deputy (usually me). If a deputy had to go on a call at night after 11 p.m. she was our only link to getting a little help. It wasn't unusual for me to go to work on Friday and not go home until Sunday. You worked from can to can't. We had a few volunteer deputies that helped out from time to time on the weekends.

Sheriff's Department Makes History

DUG DOWN INSIDE THEIR POCK-ETS—Members of the Chattooga County Sheriff's Department, and Sheriff John F r a n k McConnell are proud of their department. And it can't be said after today that they aren't proud enough to go a long way to improve it. These men wanted uniforms, and spent their own funds to obtain them. That might not sound like so much until you learn that each uniform (one hat, two trousers and three shirts) cost these men about $50 each. That's a lot of money out of any man's pay check. In doing this they also made a record, for this is the first time that the sheriff's department has had men in uniforms. (L-R)—front r o w, Deputies W. R. Coker, Robert King, J. D. Miller, Elbert Tucker; back row, Deputy G a r y McConnell, and Sheriff McConnell.

8

Later on during his administration, my dad hired the first African-American deputies, Ira Pollard and Tom Scott. It wasn't until around the 1970s when we finally got enough help to start operating the department around the clock.

We didn't have uniforms when we first went into office. It wasn't until 1966 when we finally got uniforms and then we had to pay for them ourselves. They were green pants and khaki shirts. The surrounding counties, as well as the Trion Police Department and the Georgia State Patrol, had uniforms and we wanted to be more professional so we decided it was time for uniforms. It was around 1974-75 before the county began paying for the uniforms for the sheriff's department. It was during that time that all the sheriff's departments in the state went to the same color uniforms that they still wear today.

As I mentioned, in the early 60s Chattooga County was a dry county and for that reason moonshine and bootleggers were rampantly operating throughout the county. My dad's campaign platform that he would clean up the county kept us busy. We attempted to keep that promise by destroying one still at a time. There were so many stills throughout the county that it wasn't hard to find them. In the rural areas there were trails just about everywhere you looked. Deputy Bert Tucker was amazing at finding trails to stills. You could be going down the road and Bert would say, "Stop, there's a trail." We'd stop

and sure enough there'd be a trail. We'd follow it and find a still. Sometimes they'd be in operation and other times they wouldn't.

There was more going on in the county than just moonshiners and bootleggers. The first major case we had to handle wasn't one we solved, but one we were charged with overseeing. Our involvement in the case began within a month of our going into office and involved the bludgeoning death of a 47-year-old Walker County carpet mill executive.

A LaFayette resident, Billy A. Copeland, had been murdered in Chattooga County the December before we took office in January. Thankfully, the killers were caught in South Georgia a short time later. Two West Virginia residents (Roy Dale Chatterton, age 21, and Woodrow 'Woody' Whisman, age 18) were arrested near Savannah Dec. 23, 1964, on robbery and assault charges stemming from another incident. During their incarceration, they confessed to killing Copeland and told authorities where to find him. Copeland's body was discovered in an abandoned farm house in the Haywood Valley Community in Chattooga near where it borders with Floyd County. Chatterton and Whisman were transported back to Chattooga to stand trial for his murder.

Copeland had been enroute to Rome on Dec. 18th to pick up one of his sons from college. A short distance south of Summerville on Highway 27, he came upon Chatterton and Whisman hitchhiking. Copeland stopped and gave them a ride. You have

Gary W. McConnell

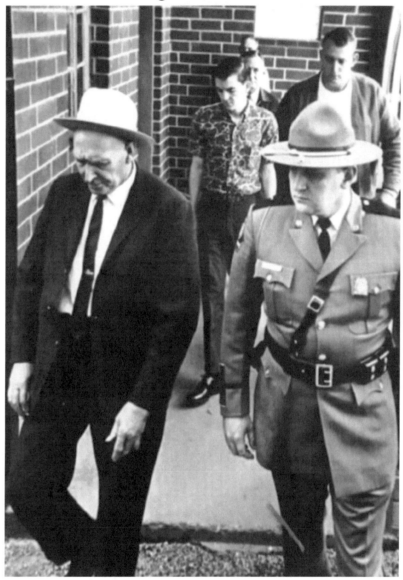

*Chattooga County Sheriff John Frank McConnell (left)
and an unidentified Georgia State Trooper (right) lead
the way as Woodrow Whisman (second from left) is taken
from the county jail to Superior Court for the 1964 slaying
of Billy Copeland of LaFayette. Officers accompanying
Whisman are Deputy Gary McConnell (beside him) and
Deputy Bert Tucker.*

to remember this was during an era when people hitchhiked a lot and it wasn't uncommon for strangers to stop and give them a lift.

They soon turned the tables on him and abducted him at knife point. When they arrived at an abandoned farm house they made him strip to his underclothing and tied him up. When Copeland continued to ask for his personal effects in his wallet, particularly photos of his family, they struck him with a plank. Taking some of

Sheriff John Frank McConnell (right) leads the way into the Chattooga County Courthouse during the murder trial of Woodrow Whisman (second from left). Deputy Gary McConnell (second from right) helps escort Whisman, along with deputy Bert Tucker (left). Whisman was charged and convicted of murdering Billy Copeland, a Walker County resident as he traveled through Chattooga enroute to Floyd County.

his clothing and car, they left Copeland tied up, gagged, and badly injured. Medical authorities would later testify that Copeland died from his head injuries.

Chatterton and Whisman weren't even here when we took office. Chief Deputy Randy Roberts and local GBI (Georgia Bureau of Investigation) Agent Jack Knott transported them back here in early January from Savannah where they had been arrested. Chatterton and I were about the same age. It was the first time I'd ever been around a murderer. He was polite, but arrogant. Whisman was more subdued, what I'd call sheepish. He was a murderer, don't misunderstand, but he was much quieter and wasn't in your face. He knew he was in a heap of trouble, I guess is a nice way to put it. Chatterton was still pretty much 'in your face'.

They appeared in Chattooga County Superior Court in February before Judge Robert E. Coker. It was the first case Judge Coker had heard. He got elected to the bench the same time my dad got elected sheriff. Normally, when we went back and forth to court, Chatterton and I were handcuffed together. He was a pretty good size guy but I was a big guy too. I'd sit him down at the table in the courtroom and he had leg irons on, as well as a version of restraint braces that you could lock. They looked kind of like knee braces but when you sat down and twisted a little knob on them, they wouldn't let you straighten your legs out. We'd put

Sheriff John Frank McConnell (left) talks with prisoner Roy Dale Chatterton (right) in the Chattooga County Jail. Chatterton was charged and convicted of murdering Billy Copeland, a LaFayette resident traveling through Chattooga enroute to Floyd County to pick up his son from college for Christmas vacation.

them on him before he left the jail. He could walk with them, but when he sat down you could lock them and then he couldn't stand up.

Whisman didn't have to wear the braces. The two murderers were different in stature. Chatterton was a pretty good size fella and was in good physical shape. He would have been a handful to deal with. He didn't give us a lot of trouble. However, one morning after he'd been sentenced to die in the electric chair, he and I had a little tit-for-tat

coming back down the stairs from the courtroom. We had a little shoving match. It didn't last long and no one was injured.

The Copeland family hired local attorney Bobby Lee Cook to help Solicitor General (now known as District Attorney) Earl Self prosecute them. At the time, the District Attorney's office didn't have any assistants, it was just Mr. Self. They (Chatterton and Whisman) beat Mr. Copeland to death with a 2 by 2 board and it had been recovered at the crime scene. One of the strange things that happened during the trial was that Bobby Lee had the 2 by 2 and Earl got down on the floor pretending to be Mr. Copeland. Bobby Lee was showing how they beat Copeland to death, but then Earl couldn't get up and we had to help him.

Chatterton and Whisman were tried separately. Both were found guilty and sentenced to die. Chatterton was sentenced shortly after 10 a.m. He had been found guilty without a recommendation of mercy by an all-male jury. It took them 50 minutes to deliberate. He was sentenced to die between 10 a.m. and 2 p.m. on Friday, March 19, 1965, at the Reidsville State Prison. A motion for a new trial stayed that execution. Chatterton's appointed attorneys were Donald Bennett, Rossville, and Dave Lomenick, LaFayette. (Years later Lomenick would become District Attorney in the same Lookout Mountain Judicial Circuit.) Whisman was also found guilty with no recommendation for mercy making a death sentence mandatory. It took

Just one of the many stills destroyed throughout the early years of the McConnell administration. It's a good example of how the stills were set up and the way they were operated.

his jury one hour and 15 minutes to deliberate.

A new trial was denied for Whisman on May 25 (1965) and Chatterton's was denied three days later. The appeals and reappearances in court continued off and on for years. Judge Coker ordered new execution dates for them to be carried out on April 10 (1968). This was the fourth time they were under a death sentence. The pair was taken back to Reidsville State Prison to await further developments.

In time both Chatterton and Whisman's sentences were overturned. After numerous parole hearings throughout the years, both men were released from prison by the parole board

despite my efforts to keep them incarcerated. My hope was that both men would at least remain in prison until Copeland's widow passed away in order to give her some peace of mind, but that didn't happen and both men were released before she died.

When we weren't busy with the courts, we were still out busting stills and serving to protect the county. During those early days of the administration, every week you'd read in the local newspaper about a number of stills that had been destroyed all over the county.

Most of the stills were made out of aluminum and sheet metal and we destroyed them by busting

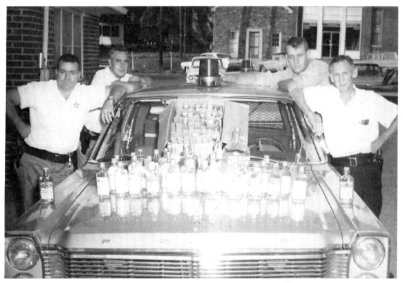

Deputies Robert King (left to right), Jack Ledford, Gary McConnell, and Bert Tucker are shown with a large amount of moonshine and bonded liquor seized in a raid. The liquor sits on one of the first patrol cars the sheriff's department had under the McConnell administration.

them with axes. Sometimes, depending on how the stills were set up, we had to use dynamite. Every once in a while, you would find a still made out of copper but those were rare as it was too expensive for the moonshiners to use. From time to time we'd also find a still that was so small it was only being used to make liquor for the owner to consume and not to sell. We destroyed those too. Some moonshiners took pride in their stills, while others didn't really care how they looked or what went into them to make the liquor. Some were operated haphazardly and really dangerous with such things as car batteries and manure mixed into the mash.

What we're talking about is a 500-gallon pot with a wood cap, a wood bottom, and sheet metal around it. We'd just take a fire ax and knock some holes in it or drop in a couple sticks of dynamite and light it. The cap sat on top, the steam came out of there, went over and there's a pipe running down to what was called a thumper. This is where it begins to change from vapor to liquid. When it starts changing, it would leave the barrel and go to what was called a coil or cooling tank.

The better stills had a copper coil to cool it off while some of them just had a car radiator to run it through. It would come out as white liquor. But most of the tanks were wooden barrels so if you took an ax and hit them, they'd cave in. Originally, we started cutting them with axes and then we started finding the stills being used again with

patches where we had busted them open. This led us to start destroying them using dynamite.

One of the most unusual things we had to happen when we were destroying a still occurred when my dad found a still inside an abandoned house. An agent with the Department of Revenue, Alcohol and Tobacco Tax Unit was with him. It was a 500 gallon still re-enforced with 1 by 6 poplar timbers. They tried to pry the timber off and tried to cut it off, but nothing was working. The agent suggested they use primer cord wrapped around the end of the still to destroy it. It was finally agreed they'd use the primer cord. My dad walked up to the agent and said, "Now Herman, under no circumstances are you to let them blow up the house."

The agent assured my dad that the type of explosive they were setting would only cut the end of the still and not damage the house. They backed away, waited for the explosion to ignite, but there was a delay in it. Just as they thought it wasn't going to light, it went off. The roof blew straight up in the air, the ceiling fell on top of the still and the walls collapsed. The house was completely demolished but the still remained intact without a scratch. They finally had to use a chain saw to destroy the still.

The still was found on land where a big confined hog farm was in operation. The house was part of the old home place, but no one was living on the property. The still had an automated auger in the bottom of it that took the mash out to feed the hogs.

It's All About The People

It was actually a push button operation, really nice. It was all copper so it was first class white liquor. We didn't charge anyone with the still because we blew the house up. We forgot about the still and they forgot about the house getting blown up. We worked out a negotiated deal there. They never went back in operation there.

We were constantly destroying stills and seizing homemade liquor (also known as moonshine or white whiskey). The stills would range anywhere from 100 gallons to 800 gallons. The largest one we found was a 4,000 gallon still we destroyed in the Subligna Community. The stills were located all over the county, not just one area. In December of 1965, we destroyed 11 stills in two days. From the time my dad went into office on Jan. 1, 1965, until Dec. 6, 1965, we had destroyed 106 stills.

3
Year Two

It was a busy time as we adjusted to being in office, working to fulfill my dad's campaign promise, and protect the residents of the county during the day-to-day problems. In February 1965, we received two patrol cars (provided by Commissioner Powell). They had top mounted red signal lights, a wire screen panel between the front and back seats, tire chains, and a siren, but no two-way radio.

Also, during February, I made some changes in my personal life. About six weeks after we'd been in office, I got married on Feb. 13, 1965, to Sylvia Rachel Waters from Summerville. We were married in the Calvary Baptist Church in Summerville. We had gone to high school together. Rachel was the daughter of Mr. and Mrs. W.D. Waters, Summerville. She was a nurse at the Riegel Hospital in Trion (GA). Rachel suffered a tremendous amount of health issues during our marriage. She also worried about the stress of my job, the long hours and safety issues I faced daily.

The sheriff's department continued to be busy and a few months later Deputy Elbert 'Bert" Tucker was named Chief Deputy succeeding

Stills were found throughout Chattooga County. Deputy Gary McConnell (left to right), Deputy Bert Tucker, and Agents Herman Evans and Denny Davis with the Department of Revenue, Alcohol and Tobacco Tax Unit are shown with one of many stills destroyed.

Randy Roberts who resigned to go into business for himself. Randy and his brother-in-law, Andrew Williams, built and operated a convenience store in the Dickeyville Community. He operated the store for about 8 or 10 years. They then sold the business and it became known as Benny's Tri-Sum Foods for many years. Randy went on to own and operate The Round Table Restaurant in the Pennville Community for many years afterwards.

The moonshiners didn't slow up. For the most part, they were peaceful people just making liquor to sell to make a living. We rarely had any serious problem when we found someone operating the stills. It wasn't anything like what you see in the movies where the moonshiners and the law

enforcement are always shooting at each other. I don't recall anyone ever getting seriously injured during a raid.

While we were destroying stills and confiscating white whiskey, we tried to treat everyone with respect. Like I said, these were basically good people doing something illegal to make a living during hard times.

We did run into some strange situations busting up stills. Everyone knew I was terrified of rattlesnakes - I still am. This one moonshiner thought he'd get me. He caught a rattlesnake and tied it across the trail going to his still. I don't know if he thought it would scare me away and we wouldn't find his still or what, but it didn't work. We found his still and destroyed it. That's probably the most serious life-threatening thing that anybody did to me.

Some of the moonshiners would put traps around their stills. They'd put trip wires to know if anybody had been in there looking at their still operation. They also had those in case we were trying to sneak up on them while they were actually running the still. The trip wires were usually a long way away from the still, say 50 to 500 feet. The trip wires were usually attached to something that would make a noise or signal the moonshiners someone was nearby. This gave them time to hide and not be arrested if it was the sheriff's department.

It's All About The People

Most of these people either made their living or subsidized their living. They weren't out to do bodily harm, at least to us.

About 98 percent of the stills were on a creek or spring branch because water was needed to make the liquor. I can only think of two or three that we got over the years that they were having to haul water to. These were very small operations.

We had a variety of other crimes we were dealing with at the same time. One example was this car thief named Gerald Dewayne Cook out of Hapeville. He'd stolen a car in Atlanta, given a ride to two Fort Gordon soldiers who were hitchhiking, and then he wrecked the car on Taylor's Ridge. He was speeding, hit a ditch and turned the car over. The soldiers were injured and Cook ran into the woods. The Warden of the Floyd County Work Camp and his dogs came up, along with the Georgia State Patrol, Chattooga County Civil Defense, and volunteers to help us catch him. We chased him for about four hours and the bloodhounds found him near Gordon McCollum's chicken houses. After he was arrested we discovered he had a broken collar bone.

A few days after that we busted one of the largest stills we'd discovered so far. It was a 4,000-gallon operation and was made with steel plates instead of aluminum. That bust was number 83 for us. We also confiscated a 1953 Ford when we destroyed the still.

Another moonshine still is being destroyed. On hand for the activities were (left to right) Deputies Bert Tucker and Gary McConnell, Sheriff John Frank McConnell, and Deputy Jack Ledford.

There was also a hit and run in front of the Dairy King that was located between Summerville and Trion. I tried to flag down a car without headlights at the scene. The car didn't stop and I gave chase. I clocked the speeding car at 100 miles per hour coming toward Summerville on Highway 27. It continued on until it got in front of the J.D. Hill Funeral Home (at the edge of downtown) where the car caught on fire. The driver jumped out and fled. The car had been stolen out of Chattanooga, TN. The driver was later caught and charged and thankfully there were no critical injuries. Deputy

Taking a quick break, deputies Gary McConnell (left) and Bert Tucker prepare to destroy another moonshine still found in the county.

Robert King hit it head on with his patrol car to stop it.

Another unusual incident happened when we blew up a still close to The Summerville News. Most of these old stills were wood burners and then they started using propane gas in these portable tanks. This was over on the creek past The News where it crosses Wildlife Lake Road. There were four or five of these medium size butane gas tanks. So, we piled all of them up, I don't know what we were thinking - apparently, we weren't thinking. We wrapped some primer cord around them, not

realizing what we were doing and what we did was blow the heads off of them where the gas comes out so they went through the woods like rockets. Just very lucky that nobody got hurt. If they've got gas in them and you knocked the top off, they'll take off on you. It was kind of scary. It was pure luck the way we did it. We weren't smart enough to know that was going to happen. We sure weren't smart enough to turn them the other way.

We also participated in breaking up a huge burglary ring that had been going on in a six-county area in which more than $11,000 in merchandise had been stolen during a six-week period. Two county residents - Ed M. Burke and Brintz Hines - along with Harold Eugene Griffith of Ringgold were arrested and charged with a number of counts of burglary and larceny. In Chattooga, the trio had burglarized Cagle's Store, Paul Holt's residence, Randy and Andy's Store, a school at Trion, Hoyt's Supermarket, a cabin on Lookout Mountain, and taken some $1,500 of copper wire from a local telephone company. They had also committed burglaries in Walker, Bartow, Gordon, Murray, and Catoosa Counties, and attempted a break-in in Floyd County. Much of the stolen merchandise was recovered at the homes of the trio.

Bootleggers sold beer and liquor (both white whiskey and bonded liquor). The bootleggers were pretty much like the moonshiners when it came to violence. They weren't dangerous criminals, but just people doing something illegal to support

their families. It wasn't unusual to go in, confiscate their beer and whiskey, arrest them, and then have them invite you to sit down and have a meal with them before they go to jail. They weren't trying to bribe you. That was just their way of saying you're doing your job and we're not mad at you. They were friendly people for the most part. Some of them were repeat offenders so you got to know them.

There was no gun play when it came to arresting bootleggers. Most of it was like a big Easter egg hunt. They'd hide it and I'd hunt it. I know that sounds silly but that's kind of the way it was. They tried to do everything they could to keep from getting caught like barring the doors so we couldn't get in, especially the ones that sold white liquor. They'd keep the door barred so they could pour the white liquor down the drain before we got in. That's where I got the nickname 'Big Foot' because I'd kick the door down. Once you got that open everything else was pretty easy.

At one time, there were some 55 places throughout the county selling or bootlegging. One of the local places was on the river outside of Trion. They had a barbecue joint and they would sell you a barbecue for 50 cents and give you a beer. He also sold white liquor and bonded liquor. They would hide the liquor in the woods. They'd take post hole diggers, dig a hole, put the gallon jugs down in the hole and keep it down there until they needed it. This was a very popular place because he did have

extremely good barbecue (and you got a cold beer) for only 50 cents. If you didn't want the beer, the barbecue was still 50 cents. They were raided many times and carried to state court. He always seemed to bring a barbecued ham with him to give to the judge just before he was sentenced. He usually got a fine which was substantial depending on how much beer and liquor was confiscated.

Donald, Big Momma, David and George, Jack, Myrtle, L.C., Ivan, Katie, Raymond - that's just what they did (bootleg). Most of them had another income. They either farmed or were in the construction business, and a couple of them worked in the mill. I can't think of but one or two of them that didn't have another income of some kind.

Some of the bootleggers had their operations set up so that you could drive up to their back door and order beer just like you do now ordering a hamburger through a fast food restaurant window. One of the bootleggers was so enterprising that he and his wife actually won a trip to Hawaii through a contest Budweiser had sponsored for businesses that sold the most beer during a certain time frame in Northwest Georgia.

Moonshine had to get from the still to the final distribution point so it was up to a middle man to do the actual transporting. He'd move it anywhere from 2 to 4 o'clock in the morning before most folks got out and about. You always heard the stories that this is where the race car drivers - the

It's All About The People

Daytona 500 type people - got their start. We had two or three guys here that had "souped-up" cars with dual false bottoms and extra tanks pretty well equipped just to haul moonshine. They were good drivers, actually fearless. There was one particular case I remember where we got after this guy on the mountain and chased him down the mountain. He got far enough ahead of us that at Shinbone Valley he ditched the car and took what's called a 'bush bond.' That's where you abandon your car and run for the hills. We checked to see whose car it was and ran him down later but couldn't arrest him right then because he'd gotten away from us. He lived here in town, and his name was Paul.

There was another guy who lived down in Holland. He made and hauled liquor. He probably had the fastest cars. There were some other folks that would haul it (moonshine) just covered under something in the bed of a pickup truck. These two particular guys had their cars equipped with false tanks, pretty well disguised, like they haul drugs today. One of the guys was good enough that he could have gone on to do some serious racing, but he didn't.

I ran into a funny situation once when I was preparing to testify in a major case. Earl Self was the Solictor General (now called District Attorny) at the time. He took me to his office to go over my testimony. Just as I was getting started, he said, "Son, you know you need to tell the truth on the stand." I said, 'Yes sir, Mother and Daddy always

taught me to tell the truth.' He said, "That's not the reason. That's a good reason, but that's not the reason I'm talking to you. The reason I'm telling you this is you're not <u>smart</u> enough to keep up with two stories." And that's pretty well the truth for anybody.

Because of my size and the fact that I was the sheriff's son, there were a good many fights in the early days when trying to arrest someone for being drunk and such. It was a challenge to a lot of folks to see if they could best me. I couldn't back down and let them get the upper hand. Sometimes I just had to bluff my way through a situation.

I remember one Sunday afternoon around 1 p.m. I was going to a friend's house to have lunch and noticed a large crowd of people gathered around a Summerville Police Department patrol car at George's Quick Mart at the north end of Summerville. So, I stopped to see what was going on and to see if I could help out. Police Chief Griffin Pledger and Patrolman L.D. McCary were attempting to arrest a gentleman in the parking lot and were having a great difficulty doing so. I went to assist with the arrest.

Once I got there, both the chief and the patrolman sat down on the ground to catch their breath and left me with the defendant. I put him in the back seat of the city patrol car after a bit of a scuffle and didn't realize that the other back door on the patrol car was open. I put him in one door and he scooted across the seat and went out the

other door. I had to run him down in the gravel parking lot and tackle him. I brought him back to the patrol car and we had another scuffle where he ended up biting me several times on my leg. Needless to say, the scuffle got more intense and he was put into the car (with the other door closed) and transported to the Chattooga County Jail. The police chief and patrolmen went back to work and I went on to lunch. Not too long ago I had a doctor ask me how long I'd had those bite marks on my leg. I told him it'd been a while.

Lawlessness was wide open when we took office and people didn't think they had to follow any of the rules of law. That was one of the biggest problems we faced. (Part of it came down to me earning their respect.) What I mean by that is they said they weren't coming and I had to show them they were. Everybody wanted to whip the sheriff's boy.

I asked somebody one day why they didn't ever jump on Tucker (who was slim built). They said everybody knows you can whip Tucker. You're a big ole boy and you're the sheriff's boy so we got something to brag about if we whip you. So I had to pretty well prove that they weren't going to (whip me). My dad told me when we started, "Don't you ever start a fight, but if they start it, don't you ever not finish it." I tried to pretty well live up to that.

I remember an incident on Sixth Street in Summerville near a local business in the black community involving city officers. The black

community was upset at the city and they had the city officers surrounded over there. It was about to get out of hand. My dad, Bert Tucker, and I went over there to help them. I don't remember the black man's name, but I was trying to put him in the patrol car. They had already broken the windshield out of the city's patrol car. I was trying to put him in the back seat of ours and I couldn't get him in. Tucker was helping as much as he could. I finally had the guy backed up against the door of the patrol car. I had a 3-cell flashlight, so I reached back just as far as I could get to hit him on the head. I did, and he didn't hardly shake his head. I thought, "Good Lord." I finally got him in the car and we started to the jail.

I was driving, Tucker was sitting in the middle and my dad was on the right in the front seat of the county car. We crossed the railroad tracks where the cotton gin used to be on First Street and I heard Tucker grunt real loud. I said, "What's wrong with you?"

He said, "Well about the time you started to hit him in the head I put my hand up there to try to shove his head in the car." My flashlight had hit Tucker's hand instead of the guy's head. Three fingers, the day he died, were still flat. I flattened his three fingers out like a pancake. I didn't hurt the black guy at all because of Tucker's hand on top of him.

With all the unusual and odd things that happened to us during the course of our work, I

was still ill-equipped for what happened when my world and my career were turned upside down on Saturday afternoon, July 8, 1967.

It was around 5 o'clock or so and Dad was going in to the house and lay down to rest a little while. I told him I was going up to Pesterfield's (a clothing store on main street). I needed to get a new belt for a friend's wedding that was coming up. I walked up to Pesterfield's to get the belt and came back. When I walked into the house mother said, "Come back here. There's something wrong with your daddy." He was laying on his bed there at the sheriff's office (in the living quarters) and he was already dead. He'd had a heart attack. We called the ambulance (the funeral homes were serving as the ambulance service at that time). I remember there was pine paneling in that room, and as far as I know it still is. I have a tendency if I get really, really, upset or mad to hit something - no body, just something. I turned around and busted one of those pine panels with my fist.

I had to take over the duties of sheriff right then. I was sworn in as sheriff about 8 o'clock that night by Ordinary Paul Weems. Within two hours after my dad was pronounced dead, I was sworn in as sheriff. That put my mother in a very unusual position. When she got up that morning, she was the wife of the sheriff. When she went to bed that night, she was the mother of the sheriff.

Clyde Erwin of Erwin Funeral Home directed dad's funeral. We came back through town in the

family car and I told Clyde to stop. I got out at the sheriff's office and went to work. For me, that was the only way I could handle it. I remember we got a call that afternoon and I answered the phone. Some lady called and had some kind of problem. She said, "I don't want to hear this shit that the sheriff just died, I need a deputy out here right now!" I thought okay I've got to get on with this. My Dad and I were awfully close. I wanted to carry on what he had started.

He died July the 8th and the special election was held on August 12th. It couldn't be less than

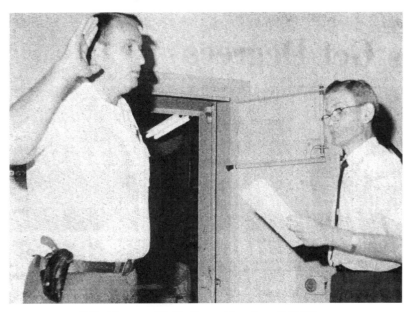

McConnell Takes Oath of Office

Gary McConnell (left) was sworn in as sheriff of Chattooga County by Ordinary Paul Weems in a brief ceremony at the courthouse Wednesday afternoon. McConnell was elected to office to fill the unexpired term of his father, the late John Frank McConnell.

30 days or more than 60 days from the vacancy I think. From July the 8th until August 12th I had to run the sheriff's office and campaign, as well as deal with the loss of my dad (and my boss). The special election was to fulfill his term which ended December 31, 1968. I wanted to continue fulfilling my dad's campaign promises to the best of my ability like we had been doing for the past two and half years.

In fact, I think destroying a still helped me win the election to continue my dad's term after he died.

Appointed Chattooga County Sheriff Gary McConnell destroys one of two large stills found in a wooded area on Lookout Mountain before the special election of August 12th.

Gary W. McConnell

I was running against five other candidates to finish my dad's term. There was Charles 'Jack' Ledford (a volunteer deputy that worked some on the weekends), William Ellenburg, J. Hairral Davis, Cecil T. Pledger, and Calvin 'Slim' Johnson. You have to remember I was only 22 years old at the time. About a week before the election I got a call from a longtime moonshiner on Lookout Mountain. He told me to come up there and bring the guy from the newspaper (the photographer). He said my daddy and I had always treated him with respect and he appreciated that. He told me I could buy ads in the newspaper, but I couldn't get one on the front page and he wanted to help me get there.

He took me to two stills on the mountain that were operational. The photographer from the newspaper made some pictures of us destroying those stills and the paper did run them on the front page two days before the election. I think that helped me win the election. Folks saw that I was carrying on my dad's promise to clean up the county of moonshiners and bootleggers. The stills belonged to the bootlegger, but you couldn't tie him to them. They were a mile, a mile and half from his house down in the woods. There was public access to them and no way to prove who owned them.

Additional photos of Sheriff John Frank McConnell and his activities as Sheriff.

Sheriff John Frank McConnell (left to right) and Deputies Gary McConnell, Robert King, and Bert Tucker are shown with beer confiscated from bootleggers throughout the county. The beer was destroyed.

Gary W. McConnell

RECOVERED BURGLARY LOOT

News-Tribune Staff Photo

This group of Northwest Georgia law enforcement officers looks over part of a mass of stolen loot recovered after the arrest of three men in Floyd County in December of 1965. The total haul in a series of area burglaries was estimated at some $11,000. The officers are (left to right) Georgia Bureau of Investigation Agent Bill Dodd of Dalton, GBI Agent R.D. Ruff of Cartersville, Floyd County Police Chief Earl Russell, Bartow Deputy Sheriff A.L. Woody, Gordon County Sheriff Hughdon Davis, Chattooga Deputy Sheriff Gary McConnell, Gordon County Detective George Hayes of Calhoun, Walker County Sheriff Ralph Jones, and Floyd Sheriff's Investigator Bill Hart.

It's All About The People

The Chattooga County Sheriff's Department and State Revenue Agent Denny Davis found this whiskey cache of 25 gallons of non-tax paid whiskey in a honeysuckle patch off the Oak Hill Road. Left to right: Davis, Sheriff John Frank McConnell, Deputy Gary McConnell, and Chief Deputy Bert Tucker.

Sheriff John Frank McConnell shown with several gallons of moonshine whiskey at the Chattooga County Jail. The illegal whiskey was confiscated from area bootleggers in his ongoing campaign to clean up the county.

4
Sheriff Gary McConnell

According to the local paper, I won the election in one of the largest landslide victories in the county's history at the time. It was almost a 10 to 1 vote over my nearest opponent. I received 2,995 votes out of 4,075 and carried all 13 precincts in the county. In Summerville, the largest precinct, I received 1,501 votes out of 2,029. Jack came in second with 352 votes, followed by William with 329, Calvin got 202, Cecil got 66, and there were several write-in candidates that received one or two votes each. The people saw I was carrying on my dad's policies so those votes were really for him. After the election, folks were very supportive. A majority of them knew I was struggling - one with his death and two with the brand-new job and being a 22-year-old with a 50-year-old's job. They couldn't have been any nicer.

That was August of 1967 and the regular election was the summer of 1968. I guess I didn't know any better than to run again for sheriff. It was how I made my living, I enjoyed it and a lot of folks encouraged me to run because they liked what I was doing based on what he (my dad) had started. We were making progress on liquor and gambling and slowing the crime rate. My only

challenger this time was Calvin 'Slim' Johnson. In the September election, I received 3,702 votes to Johnson's 2,026. The voters thought I was still doing a good job.

When my dad died, I remember at the funeral the first person that came in the door to view my dad's body was Ralph Jones, sheriff of Walker County. He pretty well took me on and tutored me as to how to be sheriff after that - the do's and don'ts and don't be stupid. He never quit doing that as long as he was sheriff. He served as sheriff until 1984.

Ralph and I became very close friends. Even to the point that when I didn't have cars, he'd loan me cars to patrol with. He guided me in the right ways to do things. That was when neither one of us had many deputies and we both worked a lot. It wasn't unusual for he and I to talk to each other at 2 o'clock in the morning about something. We were the sort of friends that if I was up at 2 or 3 o'clock in the morning working and I didn't hear him on the radio, I'd pick up the phone and call him at home and ask him what he was doing. He'd do me the same way if he happened to be out and I wasn't. We wouldn't do it every night, just occasionally to mess with the other. I remember I called him one time (I don't remember why I called) and it was 2 or 3 o'clock in the morning. I said, "Sheriff what are you doing?" He said, "I'm just sitting here on the side of the bed waiting on some fool to call me."

You always knew that if he or I either one needed help, the other one was on the way. That was especially important early on when there weren't a lot of us (law enforcement officers).

Johnny Cash got arrested in Walker County and Ralph helped get him off drugs. Cash always credited Ralph for helping him. The TV show "This Is Your Life" did a show about Johnny and Ralph was in it. Johnny Cash also came to LaFayette in 1969 thanks to Ralph and did a benefit to help the Walker County Schools.

Another thing about taking over as sheriff when my dad died was that I made Georgia history. At age 22, I was the youngest sheriff in the state's history. When I ran to fill his term in the special election and even when I ran in the regular election, I was still the youngest sheriff in the state's history. Years later as part of the Sheriffs Association, I helped draft legislation that would require anyone running for the office of sheriff in the state to be at least 25 years old, have a certain amount of training, a high school education, and be a certified law enforcement officer. Under those requirements, I could have never run for sheriff back when my dad died. There were several other officers involved in changing the law who couldn't have run for office either if that law had been in existence when they first ran. Because of that law, I'll always be the youngest sheriff ever elected in the State of Georgia.

I had been elected sheriff only 30 days in the

special election when we had our first major crime scene. Businessman L.P. 'Sonny' Wood was killed at his home in Cloudland by an unknown assailant. Sonny and his wife, Lib, operated a small grocery store on the mountain at the Georgia/Alabama state line. They had closed the store on Friday night, Sept. 7 (1967) and drove to their house which was in viewing distance of their business. When they got out of their car, Sonny was shot and killed. Lib ran into the house and called the sheriff's department. She wasn't injured. Two deputies and I responded to the scene and I asked for the GBI's help.

Here I was, a young green sheriff, trying to investigate a murder scene! Sonny was well known not only locally, but very politically involved over the state and national level. I remember I was pulling the tape to measure part of the crime scene and had to ask (at the time) United States Congressman John Davis to step aside so we could continue measuring the scene. Now folks, that's pressure on a 22-year-old sheriff. It was a long investigation and unfortunately no arrests were ever made. Following a tremendous amount of leads, years later we did link a suspect to the case through some evidence but he had already died. Lib continued to run the store and was very nervous the rest of her entire life. There is no telling how many calls we answered to her store. She was a nice lady, just very nervous and rightfully so.

George's Kwik Service, a convenience store that

Gary W. McConnell

As the newly-elected Sheriff speaking to a classroom at a local school.

was located in Summerville for years, was robbed in November of 1967. We tracked the robber to Detroit, Michigan. I went up and brought him back to stand trial.

Junior Kilgore had robbed the store and later got caught in Detroit. I flew up, took custody of him, handcuffed him and went to the airport.

It's All About The People

When we got to the airport, they wouldn't let me take him on the plane handcuffed. They made me take him back outside the airport, off of the airport property, take the handcuffs off of him and bring him back. So I guess it was safer to have him not handcuffed in the Detroit airport than it was to have him handcuffed, I don't know. That was one of their rules. They wouldn't let us board with him handcuffed.

The people of Chattooga have a generous heart for the most part. One particular time I remember is when a local family lost their home and all of their belongings in a fire. The family had carried one of their 11 children to see the doctor. While they were gone, their house caught fire and destroyed everything they owned. They were left with just the clothes they were wearing. The youngsters ranged in age from toddler to teenager.

When I learned they had nowhere to spend the night, my department and I carried them to the sheriff's office where they could have a warm place to stay overnight. This was in January and cold weather. The next morning, we got the word out about the family's situation and before long donations began arriving. There was enough to fill three pickup trucks. By that afternoon a new place for the family to live had been found and they were moved in with all their new donated items. The people really opened up their hearts to help this family in need.

In November of that year, we had a rash of

burglaries that targeted local churches and also hit a residence and a used car lot. After our investigation, we arrested two local residents and a Walker County man. The trio had worked together burglarizing several of the churches. Two of the men broke into the residence and only one of them targeted the used car lot.

STOLEN MERCHANDISE RECOVERED

Shown above are a portion of the items of stolen merchandise which the Chattooga County Sheriff's Department recovered during the last several days. The items were stolen in a series of burglaries throughout the county. Several arrests have been made by the sheriff's department in connection with the burglaries. Shown with the merchandise are Sheriff Gary McConnell (L) and Deputy Hubert Cook.

It's All About The People

One of the guys got arrested in Houston, Texas. That was when I didn't have much help so I drove out there and got him. I just drove straight out there, slept about four hours, picked him up, and drove home. His name was Bubba. I had him in court here and the judge was sentencing him. The judge asked if there was anything he wanted to say before he was sentenced. He said, "Yes sir. Whatever you do to me cannot be as bad as riding from Houston (Texas) back here with Sheriff McConnell." What he was talking about is the fact that we came back rather fast. I was gone from the county only 26 hours. (From Summerville to Houston is approximately 784 miles one way. The highway system was a bit different back then.)

We had another rash of burglaries in December of 1969 that involved breaking into residences throughout the county. We arrested several people in connection with the burglaries and recovered thousands of dollars in stolen property such as guns, small appliances, TVs and other items, as well as several hundred dollars in money. We also recovered several items stolen from a business in Floyd County. The burglars were from Chatsworth and their job with a Dalton poultry company had them traveling all over Northwest Georgia. They were in the area picking up eggs from farmers that had chicken houses. They used that to scout out the houses they broke into. There was one house in particular I remember because they broke into it twice. The last time they took the carpet, the furniture, and the light fixtures! They

were breaking into houses all over the Northwest Georgia area.

Finally, they got caught when they broke into a house in the Shinbone Valley Community near Menlo and the homeowner came home while they were there. He shot at them and they got away, but he shot a hole in their vehicle tag. He got a description of their car and called us. Sheriff Judy Poag of Murray County was in court and looked out the courthouse window in Chatsworth and saw the car go by. He ran out of the courthouse and later captured the burglar driving the car. That led to the other arrests and the recovery of the property.

I remember a murder that involved a memorable character named Bo Cramer, a very large African-American guy.

We got a call one evening to go to the Holland Community to the home of Bob Strawn. He was a big farmer in the Holland area at the time. When we arrived there, we found a 1954 Chevrolet sitting in the front yard and Bo was sitting on the front steps talking to Bob. I asked what was going on and Bo spoke up. He said, "Sheriff, I told her not to do that." So, we walked over to the car. Sitting in the backseat, leaning up against the back door was an approximately 50-year-old African-American female who was dead. She was a very small petite woman who might have weighed 90 pounds soaking wet.

It's All About The People

I looked at Bo and asked him what happened. He said, "Sheriff, I tried to get her not to do it. I said, No Baby, don't you do nothing like that. But she did it anyway."

The weapon she supposedly used was in the car with her. It was a single barrel shotgun with an extremely long barrel on it. I put it under my arm and I couldn't reach the trigger with my hand so I knew there was no humanly way possible that this very small lady could have shot herself with that shotgun. So we got the coroner down there and pronounced her dead and brought Bo to jail. We charged him with murder. While he was in jail, he turned into the man in charge in the back. He could keep order with the inmates without us having to be involved and he was pleased to do that. Bo was later sentenced for murder and served his sentence in the state penitentiary. The funny thing was what he said, "No Baby, don't you do nothing like that."

Then there was the murder that took place down in Chattoogaville near a gentleman named Henry's place. Henry was a local bootlegger. There were several houses located on his property. The gentleman by the name of Grady Maton was killed and put into a cistern on the property. Later his brother-in-law, John B. Keef of Lyerly, was arrested and charged with that murder.

I remember getting a call to check out a domestic dispute at the home of Raymond 'Bug' Kirby and his wife, Jo. Bug had a shotgun and

was threatening to shoot Jo when I arrived. He decided I was a better target and we were standing on the back porch of their home which was about a 20-foot drop off to the side so there was nowhere for me to go. I finally talked him into putting the shotgun down and we arrested him. After we got him to the jail and got him sobered up, I asked him if he had really intended to shoot me. He said if I had tried to jump off the porch he would have shot me. The Kirby family and I became good friends.

One of the more unusual things involving another sheriff was with Sheriff Mack Garrett out of Cherokee County (AL). He was a living legend in Cherokee County and around the surrounding area. We got a call that Sheriff Garrett and Alabama officers were in a chase on Highway 114 coming into Georgia from Alabama. I went down to try to cut the chase off. The car they were chasing ran off the road and into a cotton field. The guy jumped out of his car and made a run further into the cotton field where we caught him. He kept yelling, screaming and cussing. He was screaming and yelling "Just shoot me." Sheriff Garrett took out his pistol and shot into the ground about 5 feet away from the guy's head. Believe it or not, the guy didn't ask to get shot anymore. We got him up, handcuffed him, took him to jail and he was extradited back to Alabama.

Another incident that happened involved Hugh Hardison, who was a Sergeant with the Georgia State Patrol at the time. We were chasing a car - he

was in his patrol car and I was in mine - north of Trion on Highway 27. All at once the car stopped right in the middle of the road. Hugh and I split and went around the car. He went to one side and I went to the other. We both did a really good job missing the stopped car. However, when we came back in the highway we ran the sides of our two cars together, just sort of pancaked them together. The cars weren't totaled, just damaged a bit. Nobody got hurt, we both got embarrassed. The guy in the stopped car went to jail. Hugh later became the longest serving commissioner of the Department of Public Safety in Georgia's history.

Another unusual event involved a local guy who was a wrestler. A deputy was trying to arrest him in front of the old State Cafe on Commerce Street. He had jerked up a parking meter out of the ground and was after the deputy with it. I got over there to help the deputy out. I didn't know whether I could take it away from him or not. I said, "Jackie, put it down". We had a conversation then and he said, "Sheriff I think I can whip you." I said, "I'm pretty sure you can't." He stood there a minute and said, "Why don't I just lay this down and we won't ever know." I thought "Thank you, God." He said that way I can say you didn't whip me, and I didn't whip you. I thought "this is a break." This guy's standing there with a parking meter he's jerked out of the ground, and I was pretty sure he was going to be in charge. That's the sort of stuff folks don't realize you have to put up with. Most of the unusual things that happened you couldn't make

up if you tried, because they were so crazy.

The Good Lord looks after fools and idiots. One night Deputy Gerald Dempsey and I went up to Trion on Old Highway 27 on a domestic call right at the county line. The wife had reported being held against her will in the house by her husband. I knocked on the door and you could hear both of them screaming. They wouldn't open the door. It was about 11 o'clock at night and it had been raining. There's a little wooden deck front porch, no roof on it and it was wet. I had on a pair of cowboy boots. I'm alive today because my foot slipped out from under me. They wouldn't open the door so I ran back to kick the door open to get in to see about the wife and the wood floor was slick. My foot slipped out from under me just as I hit the door and I fell down. Just as I fell down, the man shot through the door with a double barrel shotgun. In other words, if I hadn't fallen down I'd probably be dead today. I got up, he came on to jail.

Another strange event occurred when a very pregnant lady had to make a decision on whether or not to come to court to try to collect child support for her child or have her baby immediately. I ended up delivering the baby for her as she lay on the couch in the judge's office in the courthouse. That was before we had EMS and all that. It was when the funeral home ran the ambulance service. By the time they got there, the baby was there too. The funny thing about it, Sam Cordle was the clerk

(of court) then. We had gotten the lady in the judge's office and started doing what we needed to do. He (Sam) said, "I'll go get some towels and hot water and stuff." I delivered the baby before the ambulance arrived and before Sam returned. Anyway, mother and baby did fine.

An unbelievable occurrence happened at a low-rent motel that was located just off Commerce Street in Summerville. Responding to a call, we found that the man in room 11 had died. Dr. Larry Howard was the Medical Examiner for Georgia at the time and traveled around the state performing autopsies. He flew to Chattooga in his private single engine plane that afternoon to conduct the autopsy. He landed his plane in the field where Wal-Mart is located today.

The autopsy was conducted at the Erwin Funeral Home. Dr. Howard had us go to the truck stop and get him an egg sandwich. He ate his lunch while doing the autopsy with his sandwich lying on the dead man's stomach. Dr. Howard determied the man had died of alcohol poisoning.

The next day we got another call from the motel that the man in room 12 had died. Same thing, bad alcohol. The next day room 13 was the same story. The guy in room 14 moved out. We never found out where the bad alcohol came from because unfortunately these guys had been drinking everything you could think of.

Back when we used to have to take people to

Milledgeville for mental problems I decided to pull a joke on Rachel, my wife. I was carrying a lady down there and you had to take another woman with you, so Rachel rode down there with me to carry this person to the mental facility. You can probably see where this is going. I had this brilliant idea when we went in, I told them it was Rachel who was supposed to be staying. I liked to have never got that straightened out. I don't mean with Rachel (that was bad enough). I mean with the hospital. They didn't think it was funny. Then I had to hear about it all the way home and for some time after we got home. I never tried that again. I thought it was a good idea, it just didn't work out the way I thought it would.

As I mentioned earlier, in August of 1968 I ran for my first full term as sheriff. Sometime after I was elected to that term, some of the merchants got together and gave me a diamond badge. There were about 25 or 30 of them. Having a diamond badge was sort of a status thing back then for sheriffs. At the time, I knew several sheriffs throughout the state that had them. It was the badge I made

the mistake of wearing when I went to see (James H.) Sloppy Floyd one day when he was state representative.

I went over there to see him about getting a raise. Sloppy had always politically supported us. I didn't even realize I had it (the diamond badge) on. I went over there and said, "I just can't make a living on what you're paying the sheriffs." It was $9,000 a year. I said, "You've gotta give us a raise." He sat there and was very attentive. He said, "Gary, you go back home and take that diamond badge off. Don't come over here telling me you can't make a living with a diamond badge on." He knew somebody gave it to me. I don't think I ever wore it out in public after that. It's in the safety deposit box at the bank now. There was one other incident with that badge and I'll explain that later on. It's a nice badge.

My family took another blow in late 1969, early 1970. My dad's mother, Nettie (Espy) McConnell, passed away. Rachel and I had gone over to my grandfather's to take him to the funeral home where my grandmother was lying in state (Dec. 18, 1969). While we were at the house Rachel went to freshen up. When she didn't return in a few minutes, I found her unconscious in the bathroom. We called the ambulance and rushed her to Floyd Hospital in Rome (GA). A brain aneurysm had erupted. She remained in a coma until Jan. 15 (1970) when she passed away.

I was with her in the hospital when we had a jail

break on Jan. 10 (1970). Six inmates overpowered Jailer Monroe Mathis and escaped. Capt. Hugh Hardison was commander of the Georgia State Patrol barracks in Rome which covered Chattooga County at that time. He came up and oversaw the capture of the prisoners for me. Four of the inmates were captured locally. The other two were apprehended in New Mexico. Wilburn Jarrett and I went out there and brought the prisoners back to jail in March (1970).

One of the escapees captured in New Mexico was named Copeland. Six to eight months prior to the escape from my jail, Copeland had escaped from a local work camp and I had arrested him. In fact, I think that was what he was in my jail for when they overpowered Monroe. Sometime during our conversation during the first capture for escape I said, "If you ever do this again, go west. I've never been out west. I'll come out there and pick you up." When he escaped the second time, Copeland got arrested in Farmington (NM). When Wilburn and I picked him up, I asked him, "How did you get off out here?" He said, "Well Sheriff, you told me if I ever escaped again to go west because you wanted to come out here. So, here I am."

We were still cracking down on beer and whiskey violations in the county in February of 1970. We conducted 17 raids throughout the county in one day using more than two dozen county, state, and federal officers. We called it Operation Dry Up. We made 73 cases for selling and possessing

beer and for selling and possessing Georgia tax paid whiskey. This came about after a month-long undercover operation by state revenue agents. We confiscated 110 cases of beer and three cases of whiskey which was turned over to the state warehouse.

Later in the month we conducted more raids that resulted in eight people being arrested on 24 separate charges. We confiscated 77 cases of beer and 33 half-pints of bonded whiskey.

A funny story involving bootleggers occurred on the west side of town when we were trying one

Law enforcement officers load cases of beer that had been seized during a series of raids conducted throughout the county. The raids resulted in 73 cases being made. It was one of the largest crackdowns on beer and whiskey in the county's history.

Just some of the places bootleggers stored their illegal beer.

of the Gentrys for possessing non-tax paid liquor in state court with a jury before Judge TJ Espy. The jury wanted to go to the scene and view the location where we found the liquor in a towel in the driveway. The judge ordered us to get a bus and carry the jury to view the crime scene. I sent a couple of deputies along with the jury to make sure there weren't any problems because that area of town had its fair share of fights, cuttings, and that sort of thing. One of the deputies was Hubert Cook. While he was there overseeing the jury, he found another 15 pints of moonshine. Needless to say, the defense attorney got really upset, came back and told the judge that we planted the liquor there to prejudice the jury which couldn't have been further from the truth. It just so happened they were still bootlegging and the liquor was where the deputy could see it. So, he got it, put it on the patrol car, took a picture of it, and brought it to me. Made perfect sense, but the judge charged me with contempt of court and fined me $200, which I had to pay out of my own pocket. At that time as sheriff I was making $750 a month so that was a pretty large fine to come out of my monthly salary, but those things happen.

The bootleggers would keep the white liquor close to the kitchen sink. We'd knock on the door, they would pour the liquor down the sink before we could get in. You had to have a little of the white liquor for evidence to prove they had it. So, I decided one day I was going to crawl under the house of one of the bootleggers before the deputies

knocked on the door. I took the drain from the sink loose, got a bucket and put it under the drain. I let them know I had everything ready. (Deputy Bert) Tucker and the deputies went and knocked on the door. The bootlegger went and poured the liquor down the sink and it came into the bucket to me. That's how you get the liquor out of the pea trap.

Over time the bootleggers got more ingenious at trying to hide their whiskey, as well as ways to get rid of it. One of the more unusual places that I found white liquor was in a church. I received some information that there was some liquor being hidden under a church just outside Trion near where a known bootlegger operated. You have to be pretty sure before you try to get a search warrant for a church looking for moonshine. We got the search warrant and found several gallons of white liquor stored in the church basement. No one from the church claimed the whiskey of course and they all said they had no knowledge of who it belonged to. There was outside access to the space so it could have been put there by anyone for safekeeping.

Most of the bootleggers had traps in their houses to hide the bonded liquor in various places. It wasn't just sitting out on the counter. You had to find the stuff. They had hidden compartments. There was this one guy, Jack, on Bill Rich Hill. We finally found his hiding place. He had a fake mantle. You took the mantle out and it (the liquor) was hidden down in the wall behind the mantle.

It's All About The People

There was one that had a window sill where you could raise the window and take the sill off then you had all the open part between the walls. A couple of them had some traps in the floor where you had to raise the carpet up. A little of it was hidden under the bed but the real bootleggers had a better hiding place than that. The white liquor, if they had a good bit, they'd usually have it hid out in the woods. They'd dig a hole, put a gallon jug down in it and then cover it up with pine straw or something. They didn't keep a lot in the house.

That's just like Donald at Trion, who would hide his liquor. He sold a lot of bonded red liquor but he'd keep maybe a dozen pints or half pints in the house and the rest of it would be out in the woods in a case or something. We raided Alvin on Menlo Highway. We went over there and raided him and couldn't find anything. I told (Deputy) Winston (Chadwick), "We just missed it. You go out and hide in the woods. I'll make a big deal about going to get a new search warrant to come back and look again." So I left, Chadwick stayed out in the woods. I hadn't much more than got out of sight, when Alvin got the case of liquor out of whereever he had it hid that we couldn't find and took it out in the woods. Winston got him when he came out of the woods.

We had some unusual things occur when dealing with bootleggers. I remember one incident involving an African-American gentleman by the name of Bernie. He had no legs and didn't wear

artificial limbs. He would collect scrap iron for a living and he also operated a little club off of Seventh Street on Friday and Saturday nights. He was sitting on a stool in the club one night when someone came in and shot him with a .22 caliber Saturday Night Special. He was carried to the hospital by the local funeral home service (this was before 911 and ambulances were operating in the county). They couldn't find the bullet he was shot with. The doctor finally determined that he was shot with the .22 pistol in the eardrum and that the bullet must have circled his brain and came back out the same hole. I remember the doctor telling him the next morning he'd have one hell of a headache. So I guess the moral of the story is if you get shot in the head, get shot with a .22 caliber pistol in the ear and hope it returns out the same hole so you only wind up with a really bad headache.

Another funny thing about Bernie involved Judge Robert E. Coker. This was when the superior court judges only came to Summerville once every six weeks. Bernie was in Superior Court before Judge Coker who had found him guilty and fined him $500. He told me to put Bernie in jail until he has paid his fine. Well, in my way of thinking, that could've been forever. So, when Judge Coker left town I decided on my own to release Bernie so he could try to get the $500. All was well and good until he ran into Judge Coker on the street in LaFayette (GA). So, the next time we had court

It's All About The People

Judge Coker was in Summerville and had me come into his office. He asked me how come Bernie Mills was on the street in LaFayette last week. My response was something like this... "Judge, he was in jail on your order and he was out of jail on my order." Then I explained the circumstances to him and he agreed that I made the right decision and didn't punish me for overruling his order.

Talking about the jail, we had some interesting characters in and out of the jail over the years and how they fit into the overall idea of jails in the late 1960s and early 70s. One was Johnny from Trion (GA). He was as nice a guy as you ever wanted to meet in your entire life. He loved to fish and was a longtime trustee at the jail. When Johnny would get out and get drunk he had a favorite saying and I'll never forget it. It was "It's a full moon tonight." Johnny's nickname was 'the lad' and he never caused anybody any trouble and he never harmed anyone except himself. He was my friend.

Homer was another guy who was his own worst enemy. He could not stay out of jail because of alcoholism. He was a trustee at the jail. At the time the parking lot was gravel and part of his job was to keep the cigarette butts picked up off the parking lot. This was when cigarettes were real popular. He was really fussy about filter cigarettes. His idea was that regular cigarettes would burn up when someone threw them down and you had to pick up all the filtered ones.

He had one unusual attribute that helped keep

him out of the chain gang. He had a tattoo on top of his bald head of a naked lady. Every time the judge started to sentence him for public drunkenness or whatever, Homer would always bow his head so the judge could see the tattoo. Every time the judge would get tickled and probably not sentence Homer to as much time as normal. But like Johnny, Homer spent a lot of time in jail because he had a serious drinking problem.

DESTROYING BEER - *Chattooga County Sheriff John Frank McConnell (center) and State Revenue Agent Herman Evans (left) watch as Courthouse Custodian Roosevelt Young destroys can after can of beer after hitting it on a pick. The 150 cases of beer had been stored in the jail.*

Sheriff Gary McConnell (left) members of his department and other helpers, destroyed 700 cases of beer behind the Chattooga County Courthouse. The beer had been confiscated in raids in the county during the last several months. Value of the beer was estimated to be more than $4,000 in case lots.

Duck was another gentleman who had a drinking problem and spent a tremendous amount of time in the jail for public drunkenness. He also served as a trustee when he was there and helped keep the jail and parking lot clean. He's another guy that never hurt anybody except himself. I remember one winter night he came to me and wanted me to put him in jail and we were full. I told him I couldn't because he hadn't committed a crime. So he goes behind the jail, walks down to the city police department, and throws a Coca-Cola bottle through their window so they would arrest him and bring him to jail. He spent the cold winter

nights in the county jail because it was the only place he had to stay.

Roosevelt Young was the County Coroner and the custodian at the Chattooga County Courthouse from the time my dad began as sheriff, and well into my own term as sheriff. Roosevelt was a very good guy, but he couldn't drive. So, when we needed the services of the coroner we'd have to go pick him up and take him to the crime scene. We'd also help him with the paperwork and that sort of thing, which was fine. Probably the most unusual thing about him was that he didn't like to be around dead people. Most of the business for the coroner is dead bodies so that was kind of a challenge, but together we made it work.

One of the things Roosevelt really enjoyed doing was destroying the alcohol we seized. When we got an order from the judge to destroy the beer and moonshine we'd seized, Roosevelt would sit on the ground in the parking lot with a pick and bust every can of beer individually. He took great pride in doing that, as well as pouring out the moonshine and bonded liquor we seized.

Roosevelt also operated the Coca-Cola machines in the courthouse. That was part of his salary. He collected buffalo nickels. He paid for his casket with buffalo nickels he had collected from the Coca-Cola machines. Harry Powell, who was County Commissioner at that time, was also a carpenter and he made Roosevelt's casket for him.

It's All About The People

There was a bit of uneasiness in June of 1970 when we had to close the county courthouse (located in the middle of downtown Summerville) for 24 hours. An unidentified man called the sheriff's office and said a bomb had been put in the courthouse.

We did a thorough search of the courthouse and found nothing. Just as a precaution we closed the building and roped off the entrances through the next day. We posted guards around the courthouse to keep anyone from going in. Thankfully, nothing came of the threat.

An unusual incident happened that year that caused an item from the county to be sent to the nation's capital. A homemade zip gun was taken from a teenager. A zip gun is a homemade weapon that can fire a .22-caliber bullet. We turned the gun over to the state and they sent it to Washington D.C to be placed on display in the nation's capital. This was at a time before very much was known about zip guns in our area.

You could say I've made some unusual arrests in my years as sheriff. There was this one time in August of 1971 when the local newspaper ran a photo of me with the headline "Unusual Arrest Made." The photo showed me with pigs. For this arrest, the criminals were 10 pigs that we had picked up running loose in the Oak Hill Community. The law says all livestock must be fenced in so it was my duty to pick up the livestock that wasn't fenced up.

Gary W. McConnell

All jails seem to have their fair share of problems with prisoners acting out. The Walker County Jail in LaFayette had a prisoner revolt in October of 1971 that caused extensive damage to the jail. Ten of those prisoners had to be transported to my jail while repairs were being made.

Apparently two prisoners began the riot by tearing lavatories and toilets out of the walls and floors. They tore the light fixtures down and destroyed them. They also put all the mattresses on one bunk and somehow managed to set them on fire causing smoke and water damage to the jail.

This all began when one deputy was on duty. He immediately called for help. Sheriff Ralph Jones, deputies, and troopers from the Georgia State Patrol responded quickly getting the situation back under control. During the fire, one of the riot ringleaders was almost asphyxiated by smoke and was revived by the firemen.

I sent our four prisoners to the Summerville City Jail and Walker sent their prisoners down here. Some of the Walker prisoners tried to continue their riot when they got here. I told them that would not be tolerated here. We used tear gas and got them under control. We didn't have any more problems out of them while they were here. They were returned to the Walker County Jail after repairs were made to the jail.

We set a record in 1971 for the largest number of

misdemeanor cases made in one year at that time. We made 3,467 cases for the year. We started 1972 with 108 misdemeanor cases made during the first 10 days of the new year.

I also did 'a first' when I hired the first female road deputy, Beth Hollis, during my early term as sheriff. The first full-time female employee of the sheriff's department was Becky Martin. Becky also went to work at GEMA when I became Director. She worked as Administrative Assistant in the Excess Property Program.

Chestnut's General Mercantile Store in Gaylesville (AL) just across the state line was robbed one night right as it was closing. Three men robbed the store at gunpoint and escaped with about $500 in cash and several cartons of cigarettes. A local resident there gave chase until they shot at his car.

We were notified they were headed in our direction in two separate cars. We apprehended them on the Menlo Highway after they tried to elude us. One of the men escaped capture at the time but was caught a short time later after hiding under a house. He had escaped from the Wayne County Prison in Jesup. We had about 25 law enforcement officers and a bloodhound looking for the fugitive.

One of the other robbers, Bobby, was from Chattooga County. He was kind of always into something and he'd known me all my life. I

arrested him here in Chattooga for the armed robbery in Gaylesville. He returned to Alabama to stand trial and decided to defend himself. I was called to testify.

Bobby kept me on the stand for over two days. He questioned me about things from the time I was

Beth Hollis and her husband, Max. Beth was the first female road deputy with the Chattooga County Sheriff's Department.

in grammar school up until the time of the armed robbery. None of the questions had anything to do with the case. The judge allowed him to ask the non-related questions since he was defending himself. The second afternoon I asked him, "Bobby what are you doing?" He said, "Sheriff it's simple. I'd rather be here in this nice courtroom than I had sitting over there in that jail." He was just as sincere about that as he could be. I asked him, "How much longer are we were going to do this (keep me on the stand)?" He said, "I think I've got about another half to three-quarters of a day for you," and he did. I was on the stand a good 15 to 16 hours but it (the testimony) was about my entire

Sheriff Gary McConnell is shown with a vast array of weapons recovered after a rash of burglaries in the county.

early life, my sheriff's career, and everything up until then simply because he didn't want to sit in jail. He was finally convicted for the armed robbery and served time in prison.

It's hard to say what people will or won't steal. We investigated the theft of a 65-foot mobile home from a local business one time. The trailer was valued at more than $9,000, and was stolen from Colonial Mobile Homes on Highway 27.

The guy was caught in Rossville and we recovered the mobile home. I was interviewing him and I asked him, "Did you get this (trailer) on Saturday or Sunday?" The mobile home lot was open the rest of the time and there was somebody there during those hours. He looked at me just as sincere as he possibly could and said, "Well Sheriff you know I didn't steal it on Sunday. It's against the law to pull a mobile home on Sunday."

Through my involvement in the Georgia Sheriff's Association, I became involved with the Georgia Sheriff's Cherokee Estates. I was elected to the board of trustees in June of 1972. I served with 11 other county sheriffs and 15 laymen throughout Georgia. We helped guide and direct the child-care institution, which the association sponsors and supports. The association started the Boys Ranch in 1964 and then later added Cherokee Estates in Dalton as an all girls facility. The facilities are called Youth Homes now.

The community here was very supportive of

the facilities. The Summerville Business and Professional Women's group used to help provide Christmas gifts for the youngsters at Cherokee Estates every year. They would make sure every child received a gift and went over to celebrate with them during the Christmas holiday. Riegel Textile (now Mount Vernon Mills) provided all the blue jeans for the facilities for a number of years. Numerous groups and organizations throughout the county gave monetary donations each year to help support and provide for the youngsters.

It (being involved with the Youth Homes) is the single best thing that a sheriff can do in this state for that group of young people – those that need that service. There are nine homes throughout the state now. If a youngster has the ability and desire now, we send them all the way through college. We have a couple of kids who are now practicing doctors. That in turn builds the program because they give back to it. There are hundreds of kids that are better off because they were there based on their situations. The majority of the funding for the homes comes from communities, small donations along with corporate sponsors.

I was interested in it because it was helping somebody and honestly, it made you feel good. Being sheriff, you deal with a lot of downtrodden type situations, good people just in bad situations. Here (with the Youth Homes) you're giving someone a helping hand. It's a good program. The youth live in homes with house parents, go to

public school, and participate in sports and other activities. They are regular kids who have a chance to live a 'normal' life they couldn't in their own homes due to difficult circumstances.

The program doesn't work for everyone, but it does give them a chance they wouldn't have had otherwise. The youth aren't sentenced there, it's a volunteer program. It's not necessarily kids that have trouble with the law. It's also for kids who are homeless or their family can't care for them for different reasons. They are downtrodden kids that need a hand up.

5
My Second Term as Sheriff

In August of 1972 I ran for my second full term as sheriff. This time I was challenged by L.D. Ragland, a retired Air Force Sergeant from Lyerly, and Roy Starkey, who was a member of the Summerville Police Department. I won the race with 2,967 votes to Ragland's 2,091 and Starkey's 513.

We continued operating the sheriff's department in the same manner we had always done, trying to serve and protect the residents of the county while ridding the area of moonshine, gambling, and bootleggers.

There are a couple of funny things I remember about living at the jail at the time and how open the jail was back then. One morning I woke up to find attorney T.J. Espy sitting on the side of my bed. He was waiting for me to wake up so I could go serve some papers for him. Another time I woke up and smelled eggs and ham cooking. I found Trooper Bill McCowen out of the Rome patrol post cooking breakfast in the kitchen. He had just made himself at home. He was used to that. He had grown up with his dad being sheriff of Polk County and had lived at the jail when he

was young. In fact, his father got shot and killed sitting on the front porch at the (Polk County) jail. I later turned the sheriff's living quarters into office space for myself and for my staff.

After Rachel had died, I gained a lot of weight. In fact, I weighed 440 pounds. Randy Roberts, who had been my dad's chief deputy and was a good friend of mine, owned The Round Table Restaurant in Pennville at the time. He and I decided to go on Weight Watchers. Randy came up with the idea that we eat every meal at his restaurant. (I believe to this day he did it to try to help me lose weight.) We wouldn't pay for it until we both decided it was time to quit and whoever lost the least would have to pay for both our meals. I certainly had more weight to lose than he did, but it finally dawned on me he was going to pay for it wholesale, I was going to pay for it whatever the going price was. I had to buckle up.

I lost 144 pounds in 40 weeks and won the bet. The reason it was successful for me was that I didn't eat anything anywhere except there. I didn't order. I just went in and he had his cook keep up with what we were supposed to eat through Weight Watchers. I just sat down and they'd bring something out and I'd eat it whether I liked it or not. I have a photo of me and the guy who played the Dodge Sheriff on TV ads at a sheriffs' convention. In the photo, we're bumping bellies when I was at my biggest (and he was a pretty big guy himself).

It's All About The People

I had to make a trip to Canada once to bring back a man who was charged with interfering with the custody of minor children. The Metropolitan Police Department of Toronto picked up James N. Mitchell for us. Mitchell was a member of the Four-Square Church which I had never heard of then or since. He was involved in a custody dispute and had kidnapped his children.

Court was going on in Ringgold so I went to see Superior Court Judge Robert E. Coker to see if we could spend the kind of money it would take for me to go after Mitchell. Judge Coker signed the order but noted that I had to carry the district attorney, Bill Self, with me for legal advice. We flew in and when we got to the Canadian border, they wouldn't let me carry my gun with me into Canada. Canada had very strict gun laws.

I explained to them why I was there, but that didn't make any difference. Finally, they said, "Sheriff it (meaning my gun) is going to be right here when you get back, but it's not going past this line." They said they would escort me and Mitchell back to right there and I could be armed and then take custody of Mitchell. They told me that until I got right there, he was in their custody and I didn't need a weapon (and I didn't get to keep mine). They were very nice about it and they escorted me right back to that line in the airport where I got my gun back and took custody of Mitchell before we returned to Chattooga County.

Marijuana was beginning to grow in popularity

Gary W. McConnell

here in late 1973. We made a record haul when the largest amount of marijuana in the department's history (at that time) was found growing on Little Sand Mountain near an abandoned farmhouse.

We found 14 patches of marijuana and each one of them was 10-foot by 10-foot in size. We also found seeds and dried leaves inside the farmhouse. The market price at the time was about $15,000. We arrested one local man and four men from Dalton in connection with the marijuana find.

The body of a 19-year-old youth, James Olin Hammond Jr., was discovered in a wooded, rural area of the county in June of 1974. He had been walking home from work when he was attacked by three young men. He worked as a bag boy at Hurley's (a grocery store) in Trion. They killed him and robbed him of $67. Our investigation led to the arrest of George Thomas Lerch Jr., 29, of Ringgold; Billy Ray Wilson; and Jess Dodson, 19, of Trion. I had to go to Buford, NC, to pick up Dodson for his part in the murder. This was a terrible case. There are a couple of things I remember about this case. They (the killers) had used a hammer to knock a hole in the teenager's skull. The hole was about the size of the opening of a drinking glass. They took a stick and stirred the boy's brains. This had happened on a logging road. During their confession, one of the killers said they had stopped on the way back and washed their hands in a mud puddle to get the blood off.

Lerch was arrested in Catoosa County. When I

picked him up I told him that I hoped he lived the rest of his life watching the blood run out of that boy's head and down the walls when he went to sleep at night. His defense made a big issue out of that when we got to court. They said the sheriff threatened to splatter his (Lerch's) blood on the wall. I said, "No sir. What I said was I hoped he got to watch the Hammond boy's blood run down his cell wall the rest of his life." They were convicted and served time in prison for what they did.

As we neared the September term of court in 1974, it was apparent there was a growing drug traffic problem in our county. We had a large number of cases involving drug abuse going to trial. We had reports coming in from residents throughout the county about the problem.

A concerted effort was being made to stop the illicit and profitable drug business in the community. I urged local residents to cooperate with the Chattooga and Trion school systems, our office, and all other law enforcement agencies to eliminate drug traffic in the county. I urged residents to let their thoughts on the drug problem be known to Superior Court Judge Robert E. Coker and Juvenile Court Judge Jerry Westbrook.

While drugs were becoming more and more of a problem in the county, we still had other problems as well. The Trion branch of the Farmers and Merchants Bank was robbed at gunpoint shortly after opening for the day's business on Nov. 22 (1974). The robber fled the bank with

an undisclosed amount of money and stole an employee's car.

A lookout for the suspect and car was put out and officers in Walker County soon gave chase. He eluded officers and abandoned the car. We later tracked the suspect down in Hamilton County, Ohio. He was Howard Tony Briscoe and later identified from a lineup as the armed robber.

I remember another bank robbery where we found the stolen money in an unusual place when we arrested one of the robbers. Huey Edwin Nelson of Summerville was one of three men who had robbed the Citizens Bank in Valley Head, AL.

We apprehended Nelson at a motel in the Gore Community in Chattooga County. He had taken the pad off the bottom of a table lamp and stuffed the stolen money into the hollow part of the lamp and replaced the pad. That might have worked well, but he didn't get all the money in the lamp and some of it was sticking out where we could see it. We recovered a portion of the $4,500 taken from the bank and more of the stolen money was recovered with the arrests of the other robbers.

We continued our efforts to crack down on the drug traffic each week. One of our busiest weeks was in early December of 1974. We made 14 arrests on drug related charges that week. They were part of 59 cases made during that time.

In addition, we had a bomb threat at a local restaurant. A man called the sheriff's office and said

It's All About The People

(Photo by Emmett Nunn)

Huey Edwin Nelson, 33, of Summerville (right) was arrested in a Summerville motel and charged with the robbery of the Citizens Bank of Valley Head, in Alabama. Chattooga County Sheriff Gary McConnell (left), along with FBI Agent Ken Patton, made the arrest.

a bomb had been taped to the lavatory in the men's restroom at Jack's, a hamburger establishment that was in the Summerville Square Shopping center at that time. The caller said a second bomb had also been placed in the restaurant and its location wouldn't be revealed unless all the money in the building was delivered to a certain location. Deputies Jon Payne and Gene Nix found the "bomb" in the restroom. I later dismantled it. A thorough search of the business failed to turn up a second device, but it did create a bit of excitement for the facility at the time.

6
Yes, Mr. President

There was a seemingly routine shoplifting incident where a young lady was arrested and spent a few hours in the county jail. Her arrest led to a most unusual conversation for me ... a phone call from the President of the United States.

In 1974 a 19-year-old Patty Hearst was reportedly kidnapped in California by a left-wing terrorist group known as the Symbionese Liberation Army (SLA). It was later believed she became a supporter of the group's cause and even took part in their illegal activities. The FBI had notified us and the surrounding law enforcement agencies that they thought Patty Hearst and a couple of other folks were living in a cabin somewhere on Lookout Mountain. This was around the height of her being kidnapped and becoming part of the group.

This incident occurred at the Piggly Wiggly Grocery Store in Trion during that period in February of 1975. She had a 24-inch iron skillet and other items hidden in her large jacket. The jacket had a pocket in the back and that's where the skillet was. We got a call about someone shoplifting and deputies went to investigate. They arrested

her and brought her to jail. There was a guy with her but he didn't have anything on him so he wasn't arrested.

At the jail, we observed that the young woman pretty well fit the description of Patty Hearst. We investigated further, called the FBI, they came up, and collectively we decided she was

President Gerald R. Ford, Jr.

U.S. National Archives and Records Administration

Patty Hearst. Later that night I got a call from the FBI director in Washington D.C. telling me it wasn't her and I needed to release her. I disagreed whether it was her or not and I disagreed on whether to release her or not. She was in my jail and I had local charges and I said no, I was not going to release her. We had a pretty friendly conversation and that was it.

About 10 minutes later I got another phone call from Washington D.C. It was President (Gerald) Ford. Of course, it was yes sir, no sir, what can we do for you and all that. He said, "I understand you have a lady there the FBI wants you to release and you're not willing to do that. You need to take

the FBI's advice and do what they ask you to do."
I said, "Mr. President I've got her for shoplifting."
He said, "Sheriff you don't understand. The FBI
thinks you should release her and you should
release her" and I did.

The young woman had all the scars, tattoos,
and everything that the flyer had described about
Patty Hearst. The flyer described a tattoo she had
between her knee and her hip and included a
picture of it. This girl had the same tattoo in the
same location. There's no question it was Patty
Hearst in anybody's mind, even the FBI agents or
they wouldn't have had the head FBI guy and the
President call and say release her. There wasn't
DNA testing back then and the FBI took custody
of her fingerprints.

We released her and that was the end of that
story. There was a lot of talk at that time that Patty
Hearst was working undercover for the FBI in the
Symbionese Liberation Army she was with. In my
mind, having to release her confirmed that she
had some connection to the FBI. I wouldn't say
she was undercover for them because I don't know
that. I know they were awfully interested in getting
her released. That was it. We never had any more
dealings with her or saw her around. It was like it
never happened. And that was the first time I ever
talked to a President.

I was surprised that it got up the ladder that
far that quickly. This was all in one night. She got
arrested around 4 or 5 o'clock in the afternoon and

this was over before midnight. She was not hateful or ugly while in custody. She was very cooperative and pleasant as anyone could be for someone getting put in jail for shoplifting. She didn't do anything to indicate she was all that important. That is one shoplifting incident I won't ever forget.

The Farmers and Merchants Bank was the target of another bank robbery in April of 1975. This time it was their Menlo branch that was robbed at gunpoint by four men. The men, armed with rifles and submachine guns, forced the bank employees and customers to lie on the floor while they gathered up the money. The search for the bank robbers went into Alabama. The getaway car was found in DeKalb County (AL) later. It had been stolen in Ohio. The investigation was turned over to the FBI.

Another unusual case we had involved a call from DeKalb County (AL). Someone had stolen a boat over there and they thought it might have

The Menlo branch of the Farmers & Merchants Bank was the scene of a bank robbery.

been brought over here. The boat was a 15-foot, flat-bottom john boat. From the investigation, we had an idea who might have taken the boat. I went to this rock house that used to be across from Trade Day on Highway 27 and there was a 15-foot john boat leaning up against the house. Come to find out, it was the stolen boat from Alabama. I talked to the folks in the house and that's where the story becomes unusual. The boat had been stolen by a man named Donnie. He had hitchhiked home with this boat. He didn't seem to think there was anything out of the ordinary hitchhiking with a stolen 15-foot boat. Apparently, motorists didn't think anything was out of the ordinary either about a man hitchhiking with a john boat.

7
Diane

Doing police work you just never know what you're going to encounter or who you're going to meet. In fact, I met my current wife because of police work. Let me clarify that, it was actually because of a traffic wreck. This meeting happened in 1975, and we married six months later.

I had gone up to attorney T.J. Espy's office on Commerce Street one day. I did that from time to time just to get away from the sheriff's department for a few minutes. While I was there that day, there was a wreck right outside the office and I went out to see if I could assist the Summerville Police Department in any way. The wreck was between a local lady and this woman from Walker County (GA). The wreck was worked and I found out this lady from LaFayette was named Diane. I also got her number and called her several days later for a date.

She was living with her parents at the time having just moved back here from Texas. She was actually friends with a lady I had dated for a while months earlier but wasn't any more and she had come down to see her.

We dated for a while and got married sometime

Walker County Sheriff Ralph Jones (left) had some help in taking us to jail after Diane and I married. Chattooga County deputies Winston Chadwick (second from left) and Gerald Dempsey (second from right), along with Wilburn Jarrett, helped Ralph get his revenge for when I had taken him and his new bride to the Chattooga County Jail.

Gary W. McConnell

Diane and me in the Walker County Jail after our wedding.

later on Sept. 19, 1975. We said, 'I do,' walked out of the church and went straight to jail courtesy of Walker County Sheriff Ralph Jones. There's a story behind that. Guess you could say Ralph was just paying me back for something I had done to him the year before. Ralph had gotten remarried at the Methodist Church in LaFayette. When he and his bride, Mary, said I do and turned to walk down the aisle, I stood up about half way down the aisle and took them out of the church and to my jail.

Diane and I kind of thought we could get in and get out of church without anyone outside the family knowing. It wasn't a big wedding at all. We said our vows and got out of the church. I said something like 'we've got it made.' But we didn't. Ralph had the whole church surrounded. So he took us to his jail. We spent about 30 or 40 minutes there and then he released us. It was his payback for what I'd done earlier.

8
New Hire

We had a "first" recorded for the sheriff's department in September of 1975. The Rev. Joe K. Tanner was selected to serve as the department's chaplain. The Baptist minister was appointed to lend spiritual and moral support through the department. It was the first time a chaplain had been on duty with the sheriff's department.

He assisted the department and their families with any spiritual needs and ministered to residents involved in crisis as the need arose. The Rev. Tanner was also included in an edition of the magazine "Outstanding Young Men of America" publication at the same time.

9
Local Commissioner

Sometimes you have to pursue cases that are difficult because of their sensitive nature. I was faced with one such case when I had to arrest County Commissioner Harry Powell. There were allegations that he had mistreated prisoners at the county work camp.

The Powells and the McConnells went back several generations living in the same community. Harry had been warden of the County Work Camp when my dad took over. When dad was elected sheriff, Harry was elected county commissioner. The commissioner's office held the purse strings for the sheriff's department so we were constantly interacting. Over the years (through my dad's administration and then my own), there was some conflict between the two agencies as there is in any county.

When the allegations against Harry were presented to me, I had no choice but to pursue them as I would have regardless who they were against. It wasn't done in malice against him even though the day my dad died, Harry prorated his pay for the day he died. When he gave my mother dad's check for that week, he only paid up until

the hour dad died instead of the entire day.

Harry was indicted in August of 1975 on five morals charges and released on a $2,000 bond by Judge Paul Painter. The charges included five counts of sodomy with inmates at the County Work Camp, as well as four aggravated sodomy and one count of sodomy involving other inmates. He pleaded not guilty later that month. He was later found not guilty when the case when to trial. I did my job to arrest him for the charges and the court did its job when they released him with a not guilty verdict.

10
Some of the Horrible Things Families Do to Each Other

Acts of violence people commit against each other are hard to understand sometimes. That's especially true when children are involved. There was an incident where a woman left her baby on top of her car and drove off. This was when we still had a hospital here.

The lady lived on Orchard Hill Road. She sat her baby, who was about 12 or 15 months old, on top of her car, forgot about it and drove to town. The baby fell off and wound up in the hospital in pretty bad shape. Let's just say I had strong feelings against this woman. She didn't even know she sat him up there. She said I don't know how he got up there. Well, he sure didn't crawl up there on his own.

One unusual killing I remember investigating involved two brothers that lived together out on the mountain right at the Chattooga/Walker County line. They stayed drunk all the time.

They got into a fight and one of them grabbed a sling blade, while the other one grabbed an ax. The brother with the ax lived. There wasn't anything

Gary W. McConnell

Shown with one of the vehicles recovered in a huge theft ring that covered three states.

that built up to the killing, it was just the spur of the moment and they were both drunk. What made it unusual was the ax and the sling blade were used as weapons.

We broke up a three-state auto theft ring in April of 1976. From that we recovered 13 cars and trucks with an estimated retail value of $50,000. The operation involved five counties in three states. The vehicles were recovered from Ideal Motor Company in Summerville.

At that time, it was one of the largest auto theft rings ever broken up in the county and northwest Georgia. The vehicles were stolen from Rome, Ringgold, Chattanooga (TN), and Trenton.

I was deeply honored with the Distinguished Humanitarian Award in August of 1976 for my "outstanding work" with the Cherokee Estates Boys Ranch in Dalton and the Sheriff's Boys Ranch in Hahira. At the same time I was elected secretary-treasurer of the Georgia Sheriff's Association. I was a member of the board of directors of both groups.

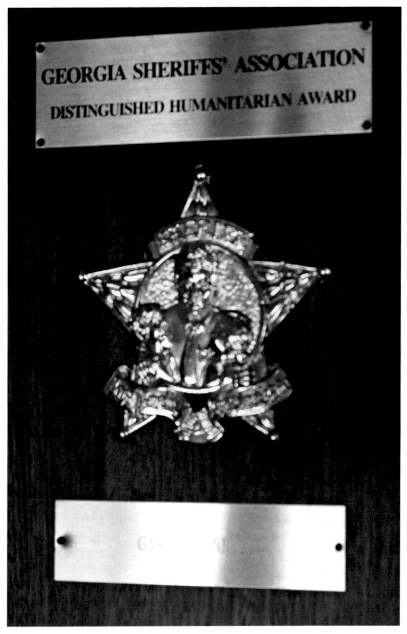

Humanitarian Award from the Georgia Sheriff's Association for my "outstanding work" with the Cherokee Estates Boys Ranch in Dalton and the Sheriff's Boys Ranch in Hahira.

It's All About The People

Authorities Recover Several Tractors

The Chattooga County Sheriff's Department, as of Tuesday morning, had recovered eight Ford tractors (above) allegedly stolen over a period of months from the Fulton/Cobb County area. Deputies began recovering the new tractors last Thursday. According to authorities, some of the tractors were concealed, while others were not. More tractors are expected to be recovered and arrests are expected to be made in the near future, said authorities.

Photos and cutline as it appeared in The Summerville News

11
My Third Term Election

My next run for office was in August of 1976. This time L.D. Ragland ran against me again, along with Gene Nix and James Pierce. Nix and Pierce later became police officers. In the August primary I received 2,971 votes to Ragland's 2,622. Nix received 371 and Pierce got 178. Because no one received the majority vote, we had a run-off election in September between me and Ragland.

Three of the candidates in the primary election are shown greeting a voter outside the Chattooga County Courthouse. Long lines of voters streamed in to vote. Candidates shown are Sheriff Gary McConnell (left to right), Sole County Commissioner Pete Denson, and County Coroner Earle Rainwater.

It's All About The People

This time around Ragland got 3,209 votes to my 3,099 votes. I got beat by 110 votes (even after a recount).

I guess you could say I had done it to myself. I had gotten to the place where I thought it was my county and I couldn't be beat. I had been in office since 1965 in one capacity or another. Ragland took over the office of sheriff in January 1977 and I went into private business for myself. I opened a farm supply and hardware store in Summerville. The business did well the first couple of years. I enjoyed what I was doing, I got to be with my family more, and I enjoyed my farm. Then a strange thing happed that caused me to get back into the political arena.

The economy had taken a turn, especially where farms and farmers were concerned, and a good many farms in the area went under. Business for us had slowed too. About two years in to my new venture, we had a burglary and about $10,000 worth of items were taken. Ragland and his deputies caught the culprits, arrested them and got back most of the stuff that had been stolen. Having been in law enforcement for so many years, I know that it can sometimes be a thankless job. I decided, with the best of intentions, to call the sheriff and thank him for what he'd done. I called and said my thanks, but the reaction I got was a complete surprise. Let's just say I didn't appreciate his remark about my good intention. At that moment, I informed him I would be running

against him at the next election. It came out of my mouth just that quick. I guess it was always in the back of my mind but I really didn't have any intentions of running against him until I called to thank him.

From that day forward, I started campaigning to run for sheriff again. I never looked back. Once I decided, it was easy from there on. When you're campaigning, you get to see a lot of people you don't normally get to see. Campaigning is hard work. You want to visit with those working the mills but you want to see them before they go to work, not when they're coming out. So, you have to time your stops at the mills to coincide with the shift changes. You catch this mill at 7, 3, and 11 and another mill at 8, 4, and 12. Most people are pleasant enough but of course a few aren't.

12
My Third Term As Sheriff

The primary was in August 1980 and I won with an overwhelming victory. According to the local paper, it was the largest election turnout in the county's history (at that time). There were three of us in the race - me, Ragland and William 'Bill' Bell. At the close of the election Bell received 325 votes (4.6 percent), Ragland got 2,684 votes (38.3 percent) and I received 4,000 votes (57 percent). In the November election I received 5,160 votes, Ragland got 29 write-ins, and four other residents got a total of 8 write-in votes. I think the residents of the county were happy to have me back in office. They knew my commitment for law and order and that I'd do my best to live up to that promise.

The job of being sheriff doesn't end at 5 every day or even when you leave the office regardless of the time of day. It's a job where you're always working (even when you're off) and sometimes parts of the job come home to touch your family regardless what you do.

13
My Family

In 1979 we welcomed a wonderful addition to our family, a daughter, Rebecca Michelle. A few years later, a man threatened to kill her. At the time I didn't tell my wife, Diane, because I didn't want to worry her. The man was in jail and he and I had had a confrontation that was pretty serious. He threatened to kill Becky and needless to say our confrontation got more serious. Somehow the local newspaper found out about the threat and ran a story on the front page. When I found out about the story in the paper, they had already printed the paper for that week. I went over to the newspaper office and tried to buy every paper they had, but they wouldn't sell them to me. So I had to go home and tell Diane about the threat before she could read it in the paper. She was upset with me. I later got sued over that confrontation in the jail, but I won.

Diane also got mad at me for not telling her about taking Becky to an armed robbery when she was a youngster. I had picked her up from school and got a call that there had been an armed robbery at a package store on the Back Penn Road in the Pennville Community. The robbery had already

happened, so I didn't see any harm in Becky going with me. We later caught the suspect.

There was another incident where someone had threatened to kill not only Becky, but me and Diane as well. A guy had shot a Department of Family and Children Services employee in their parking lot over a custody issue with his children. I arrested him and he was sent to prison for several years. When he got out, he started calling the house threatening us. He said he knew where we went to church, how we took Becky to school and such. We took extra precautions, watched our surroundings, and altered our routines. That's one thing people forget about. You tend to follow the same routine day in and day out so if someone is out to harm you, they can learn your patterns and find where you are most vulnerable. Nothing ever came of the threat against the three of us. This story just goes to show even law enforcement in small towns face the threat of danger for themselves and their families.

I mentioned earlier about the Youth Homes sponsored by the Georgia Sheriff's Association. I'll tell you how much I think of the program. When Becky was little, Diane and I had agreed that if we both got killed at the same time, we wanted Becky to go to the Youth Homes. That's about the best recommendation I can give for the program.

Growing up around law enforcement all of her life, Becky decided to serve the public in a slightly different way. After graduating from Trion

High School, she went to college and then law school. She now lives in Cobb County (GA) and practices civil law in the greater Atlanta area. Our granddaughter, McKenna, is nicknamed "Mac" and we are extremely proud of both of our girls.

It wasn't always a direct threat that you faced. One time we conducted a number of big drug raids one weekend. The next morning, I found 17 head of my cattle shot in a pasture I was leasing. Another time, we worked with the Department of Natural Resources to make some spotlighting arrests. We were having a lot of complaints on spotlighting deer and we were making a concentrated effort on that. We had arrested several guys. The following weekend, the heads and hides of three dead deer were left in the driveway to my house.

14
Changing Times

Before I went out of office in 1977, beer had been legalized in the county so that had put a hardship on the moonshiners and bootleggers. We were starting to find more marijuana growing throughout the county.

The Chattooga County Sheriff's Department confiscated marijuana plants northwest of Summerville. Deputies Gerald Dempsey and Johnny Bass are shown with some of the plants.

When I went back in office in 1981, we were faced with even more marijuana growing, while pills and other drugs were starting to make a bigger appearance in the county, as well. Finding marijuana is a bit harder to locate than stills.

You have to remember, stills had to be located near water to be operational and the trails in to them were used more often (the still operations had to be watched closer by the moonshiners). People growing marijuana don't have to go back and forth to their patches every day so their trails aren't as easy to find. Because of the color of the foliage, it's easier to hide a few marijuana plants in plain sight almost.

The best way to locate marijuana patches is from the air. The green of the plants is different from normal vegetation. The green of the plants is more vibrant than regular vegetation. It just stands out, so to speak. We began working with the Governor's Drug Task Force using their helicopters and pilots to spot marijuana growing throughout the county. The pilots would locate the marijuana patches and radio directions to officers on the ground on how to get to the plants. Once at the plants, officers would use machetes and such to cut the plants down.

We'd haul the plants back to the office and then destroy them in the furnace of a local textile plant. Occasionally we'd catch someone at a field or there would be enough evidence leading back to a residence from the plants so that we could

make an arrest. You couldn't always just arrest the landowner because sometimes patches were grown on people's property without them ever realizing it. This practice was happening particularly if a landowner had some wooded property they never visited.

Dealing with people growing marijuana was a bit different than dealing with moonshiners and bootleggers. For one thing, there was much more money involved. If you raided a moonshiner and destroyed his still, chances are he'd be back in business in three or four weeks likely in a different area. If you found a marijuana patch and destroyed it, the grower had to wait until the next growing season to have a crop. They were out all that money and no way to recoup it.

15
Personal Service

Times had begun to change. Personally, I had changed too. I was a different sheriff when I came back the second stint. I looked at it differently because times had already started changing before I left. We had transitioned from liquor to drugs. We were tearing up tremendous amounts of marijuana before I left so that put a different spin on the issues we were having to deal with. And when I got defeated, it gave me more of a healthy respect for the political process. I had gotten arrogant and thought it (the sheriff's job) was mine. I had also had to do some tough criminal investigations that had an effect on me.

When I came back, I wanted back because of me. The first 10 years were because of my dad. Now the issues a were a little bit different. I had more resources and had more influence with the judges and other people. The political environment was better and I had a better understanding of real life after being in business for myself. I guess you could say I understood people's struggles better. I understood them the first time, but I had lived them the second time. The people of the county had a different view of me also. It seemed that they were glad I was back. That's not a shot at the

sheriff before my second administration. I think they understood and appreciated my commitment to the county better than they did before.

It was my administration the second time, but I continued the same policies my dad had taught me. They're still in me today. One of the things you have to have to be successful in the sheriff's office is a good working relationship with not only other law enforcement agencies, but the courts and the court systems. Enforcing the law is just one prong of the criminal justice system. You've got to have respect and trust. Like with the courts in particular, you've got to always be up front with them. Even if you do your job, when you don't have that cooperation with the courts, it doesn't go any further. A lot of it comes down to credibility.

On my return to office in 1981, I became more active in statewide issues. I had been elected Secretary-Treasurer of the Georgia Sheriff's Association in 1976. When I lost the election, I resigned that post. When I went back in office I was elected Secretary-Treasurer again in 1982. I also headed up 2 or 3 study committees for the state on public safety law enforcement-type issues. I went on to serve on the Board of Public Safety which oversees the state patrol, GBI, and the training center. I also served on POST (Peace Officers and Standard Training) Council.

I guess my area of influence had expanded. Being involved in these activities helped give the county more access to available projects,

programs, resources and funds we may not have known about otherwise. By being active in these organizations, I wasn't less interested in the county and the well-being of the residents. In fact, I was just as concerned as always and this was another way to continue to help protect and provide for the residents.

I was pursuing avenues to help bring resources and programs home. Over time this led to the county getting Hays Prison, the crime lab, a new school at Trion, a water line to Menlo, a water line tying Trion and Summerville together and got the (Chattooga) river cleaned out just to name a few of the projects while I was sheriff (and as part of my later career).

One major issue I had to deal with when I returned to office was an overcrowded jail because the state wasn't picking up inmates who had been sentenced to prison. Shortly, a lawsuit was filed by an inmate concerning the overcrowding and rights violations. This issue went on for several months back and forth in the court system.

Meanwhile, I began a program for local youngsters that I'm still very proud of initiating. The Junior Deputies Program began in October of 1981 and focused on all sixth graders in the county. We met once a month with the sixth graders in all five area schools. The meetings were about 50 minutes long and were held during school hours.

We presented numerous programs for the

youngsters throughout the year teaching them safety issues. We also held Bike Road-deos teaching bicycle safety and gave away a number of bicycles. The bicycle Road-deos were held in the parking lot of the Chattooga High School. Awards were given to the first, second, third, and fourth place boy and girl winners from each school. The winners of the bicycle giveaways were selected from a hat containing all the contestant names

A boy's and a girl's bicycle were given away Saturday afternoon during the Bicycle Road-deos, sponsored by Sheriff Gary McConnell. Winning the girl's bicycle was Stephanie Wooten (left) from Lyerly Elementary, while James Holbrook (right) from Pennville Elementary won the boy's bicycle. Mary Katherine Camp of the sheriff's department assisted Sheriff McConnell in organizing the road-deo for members of the Junior Deputy Sheriff's League.

Photo courtesy of The Summerville News

Sheriff Gary McConnell (left) with Deputy Frank "Deputy Dawg" Sumner (right) of Dougherty County during one of the numerous drug programs presented for the Chattooga County School system and the community.

and didn't have anything to do with whether they received an award or not.

We also had Deputy Frank Sumner from Albany (GA) to present his "Deputy Dawg" program to the youngsters. Sumner had a drug trailer set up at each of the programs that contained a display of some 9,000 case items (evidence) that went along with the drug operation speeches he gave. He also presented Operation Drug Alert programs to the general public as well. Sumner normally gave a 40 to 50-minute speech on drug abuse.

We were doing the Junior Deputy Program and we were having many drugs (coming into the

county). We were trying to warn folks back then (early 80s) about the drug epidemic coming.

The Junior Deputy Program was trying to help address that and Deputy Dawg was a vital part of our drug program because he had so much experience and had such a good display. He talked well with the community and youngsters. When he would come, we would do not only the school programs, but also nighttime community-type programs too. Deputy Dawg coming to the county was a courtesy of Sheriff Lamar Stewart of Dougherty County in Albany at no charge. We covered the cost of him having somewhere to stay, but his salary and travel were covered by Dougherty County.

The entire Junior Deputy Program was funded through donations. It was a big hit with the kids. Even today I have people stop me and tell me how much they enjoyed participating in the program.

Drug busts continued as the problem grew locally and nationally. While some people still hadn't seen an actual marijuana plant, it was growing in popularity as a favorite drug of choice. In one raid we netted an estimated $374,000 in illicit drugs, mostly marijuana, that led to 60 arrests. One man had given a marijuana plant to his mother as a gift. She thought it was a pretty house plant and had it in her living room caring for it.

One year we led the state in pounds of marijuana seized working with the Governor's Drug Task

Law Enforcement Officers involved in one of the largest drug raids in Chattooga County's history were (left to right) Georgia State Troopers Bill Pledger, David Eury, and Joe Gossett; Chattooga Deputy Greg Latta; Trion Police Chief David Starkey; Chattooga Sheriff Gary McConnell; and Chattooga Deputy Charlie Starkey.

Force using helicopters to help locate the plants. With more drug raids, we also began to confiscate vehicles that were involved. Following one six-month undercover operation, we arrested 22 people during a seven-hour bust on 64 various charges and seized 12 vehicles.

Joe Frank Harris was governor of Georgia as the popularity of marijuana continued to rise. The state and state law enforcement officials were getting a lot of heat about using paraquat (Agent Orange) to help rid the state of marijuana. In South Georgia where they had more open land,

they were spraying the paraquat on the marijuana crops. While I was sheriff, I was also a farmer growing soybeans and we had used paraquat in farm management.

I was at a sheriffs' conference in Jekyll Island when Gov. Harris called and wanted me to come to Atlanta to be with him at a press conference. He wanted me to talk about how we (farmers) used the paraquat around our crops. I told him I was at Jekyll and couldn't get to Atlanta in time for the press conference. He said he would send a plane for me and then send me back to Jekyll when the press conference was over.

At that time the Georgia State Patrol had only one fixed wing airplane, a small one. Pilot Tommy Shaw flew down to Jekyll and picked me up at the Jekyll Airport, which is a small state operated facility. I got in the plane and we took off for Atlanta. We got up a couple thousand feet and Tommy reached over and started pecking on the gauges. I said, "What are you doing?" He said, "We're out of gas."

About that time, the plane quit running. He turned the plane and said, "We can glide back into the airport. We're still close enough to it." So we got back to the airport and landed without crashing. There wasn't anyone at the airport, but there was a fuel truck there. We hotwired the truck and got enough fuel to get us to Atlanta and to the press conference. Fuel is something you would think should be checked in a plane before you fly

somewhere to pick someone up.

We conducted the largest drug bust in the county's history netting 22 arrests on 64 various drug/alcohol-related charges and confiscation of

Talking with Georgia Gov. Joe Frank Harris (left) during one of his visits to Chattooga County during his administration.

an estimated $374,000 in drugs in early 1982. The round-up was the climax of a six-month-long undercover operation in Chattooga. By the time all was said and done, some 100 indictments were handed down by the Grand Jury in connection with the operation. The bust lasted seven hours and involved several law enforcement agencies. A total of 12 vehicles were also seized in connection with the operation.

We were still dealing with the overcrowded jail situation when a unique opportunity arose. Floyd County had a dedication ceremony for the new jail they had just built in 1982. I attended and afterwards had lunch with Dave Evans, director of the Department of Corrections; along with our local County Commissioner Pete Denson; Floyd County Sheriff Bill Hart; and a number of other people. The subject of prisons came up and I asked what it would take to get a state prison in our area. Evans explained it would take public support and a location to get things started. I came home and put an advisory board together of local residents to check the pulse of the public on having a prison here. We found a suitable location and with the support of the community we pursued the project. The outcome was the Forest Hays State Prison in the Pennville Community north of Summerville which was open to take inmates in November of 1990.

Gary W. McConnell

Sheriff Gary McConnell shown with just a small portion of the marijuana harvested during a single day's search in Chattooga County.

16
Evil

Throughout my law enforcement career, I've had to deal with death and murder. It's a sad part of the job. While I investigated numerous murders during my first administration, several cases during my second administration gained greater attention. It wasn't that the earlier cases weren't as important, it was just that the media attention began to have more of an impact during the second administration. We were dealing with not just local media, but area media outlets

Photos of Alvin Neelley and his wife, Judith Ann, as they looked at the time of their arrest in 1982.

Nineteen-year-old Judith Ann Neelley was transported to the Chattooga County Jail from death row in Alabama. Mrs. Neelley, escorted by Sheriff Gary McConnell, was brought to Chattooga County to stand trial for the October 1982 murder of 23-year-old Janice Kay Chapman. Represented by Summerville attorneys Bobby Lee Cook Jr. and Albert Palmour, Judith Ann Neelley was scheduled to stand trial but plead guilty to the murder in order to avoid another death penalty trial.

from surrounding metro cities and that in turn sometimes led to even more attention outside the county.

One of the more publicized cases involved a Tennessee couple who murdered a Floyd County (GA) woman whose body was found in the Haywood Valley Community of Chattooga in October of 1982. In fact, the murder victim was discovered not far from where Billy Copeland

It's All About The People

Judith Ann Neelley in an Alabama prison

had been murdered in 1964. The couple's crimes covered a number of states, so media attention was high.

The couple, 29-year-old Alvin Neelley and his 18-year-old wife, Judith Ann Neelley, killed 23-year-old Janice Kay Chapman of Rome. They were also charged with shooting Ms. Chapman's common-law husband, John Hancock, in Gordon County (GA). Fortunately, he survived. To compound their case, the couple kidnapped Lisa Ann Millican, a 13-year-old girl from a Rome shopping mall. They brutally murdered her and dumped her body in the Little River Canyon in neighboring Alabama. There were also a string of brutal murders and other charges associated with the couple in other states.

The Neelleys were arrested in Murfreesboro, TN, for attempting to pass fraudulent money orders there. The couple's 2-year-old twins were with them when they were arrested. It turns out

the youngsters had been with them during the killings too. The twins were turned over to Judith's parents who lived in Murfreesboro. Tennessee authorities also confiscated five weapons and two vehicles when the couple was arrested.

The Neelleys were connected to the killing in Chattooga through descriptions given by Hancock. After questioning them, Floyd County authorities (where Ms. Chapman had been taken from) began searching for her body. We determined that Ms. Chapman's body had actually been left in Chattooga near the Chattooga/Floyd county line.

We soon located her body in some undergrowth in the Haywood Valley Community. Ms. Chapman, who had been missing 12 days, had been shot three times, once in the back and twice in the chest with a .38-caliber pistol. Her badly decomposed body was found fully clothed lying on her back on the bank of the Armuchee Creek.

Ms. Chapman and Hancock were walking home when they accepted a ride with Judith. Rather than taking them home, she met up with Alvin and they all drove around. In Gordon County, Hancock was marched into the woods, shot in the back and left for dead. He later managed to make his way to a road where a truck driver helped him get medical attention.

The Millican teenager was on a shopping trip to the Riverbend Mall with a group of other youngsters from the Ethel Harpst Home in

Judith Ann Neelley in an Alabama prison

Cedartown (GA) when she disappeared. The home took care of abused and deprived children. A few days after her disappearance, police in Rome and DeKalb County (AL), as well as a Rome radio station, received calls from a woman telling them where to find the teen's body. Hancock later identified the taped voice as the woman who shot him (Judith Neelley).

The teen's body was found on a cliff in Little River Canyon about 30 miles from Rome. She had been shot once in the back of the head with a .38-caliber pistol. It was also determined, after the autopsy, that Drano had been injected into the teen's veins prior to her being shot.

The recovered bullets from Ms. Chapman were matched to one of the guns discovered in

the Neelleys' cars. The gun was also linked to the death of Lisa Ann Millican.

Judith's trial began on March 7, 1983 in DeKalb County (AL) for the teenager's murder. Shortly before the trial began, Judith gave birth to her third child while behind bars. Her twins had been born while she was in the Rome Youth Detention Center a number of years before. Following a six-week trial, Judith was convicted in DeKalb County (AL) for the murder of the teenager. The jury recommended life in prison without the possibility of parole. In capital murder cases, however, the judge has the final say on the sentencing.

Presiding Judge Randall Cole overruled the jury and sentenced Judith to die in Alabama's electric chair. At 18 years old, Judith became the youngest woman sentenced to death in the United States. To avoid another death penalty trial, Judith returned to Chattooga County where she pleaded guilty to Ms. Chapman's murder and was sentenced to life in prison. If she is ever paroled in Alabama, she'll be transferred to Georgia to fulfill her sentence here.

On March 15, 1999, just days away from her execution date, Alabama's departing Governor Fob James commuted Judith's sentence to life in prison. Met with controversy, James cited that the jury wanted to sentence her to life in prison but was overruled. Judith is incarcerated in the Julia Tutwiler Prison for Women in Wetumpka, AL, where she has spent most of her time since being

convicted.

Alvin plead guilty to murder and kidnapping charges of Ms. Chapman and wasn't tried for the murder of the teen. He was sentenced to life in prison. He went on to file a $100,000 lawsuit against me alleging we withheld medical attention from him until he confessed to his involvement in the murder/kidnapping case. U.S. District Court Judge Harold Murphy dismissed the lawsuit in May of 1984. Alvin died in the Bostick State Prison in Hardwick (GA) in 2005.

Two months after the Neelley case began, we had another brutal murder to investigate. This one, due to the sensational elements of it, not only gained national media coverage, but also international attention.

Sheriff Deputies Steve Gilreath (right) and Bert Tucker remove one of the bodies from inside Corpsewood. Looking on is Deputy Charlie Starkey as Sheriff Gary McConnell (left) oversees the crime scene.

Gary W. McConnell

A former Chicago pharmacology professor, 56-year-old Charles Scudder, and his companion, 44-year-old Joey Odom, were brutally murdered in their home that they called Corpsewood in the Mountain View Community outside of Trion (GA) on Dec. 12, 1982. Samuel Tony West, 21, and Kenneth Avery Brock, 17, also known as Kenneth Avery Lowrance, were charged with the murders. Due to Scudder and Odoms' unique lifestyle, as well as talk of devil worship, homosexuality, and drugs, national media attention to the story exploded. Then West and Brock were linked to the execution-style slaying of a Naval officer at a rest stop in Mississippi and the story gained even more attention.

The "chicken coop" building (above) on the Corpsewood Estate located near the main house. The building was used for housing fowl, canned goods, and entertaining visitors on the top floor of the three-story structure.

It's All About The People

The night of the murder, Scudder and Odom were visited by three men and a woman. The group had gone to drink wine with the two men. The four were met by Scudder who got some homemade wine and took the group to a small three-story outbuilding near the house. They all climbed the ladder to the top floor referred to as the 'pink room' for entertaining guests.

The woman and one of the men wanted to leave but were talked into staying. It was told the group had inhaled a mixture of paint thinner, glue and alcohol called 'Toot-A-Loo.' Afterwards West pulled a knife on the professor and they bound his hands and gagged him with strips from a sheet.

Sheriff Gary McConnell (right) talks with Chief Investigator Tony Gilleland (third from left) and others outside the home of Charles Scudder and Joey Odom following their murders.

Brock left the guest room, went to the house, and a number of shots were heard. Brock returned to the guest room and then everyone left going to the house. When they went into the house they saw Odom lying on the kitchen floor. The professor was marched into the living room and asked about money in the house. Scudder was then shot and the house ransacked. When the group left, the professor had been shot five times, Odom had been shot three times in the head and the men's two Old English Mastiffs had also been killed, all with a .22-caliber weapon. Four pillowcases of items, along with Scudder's jeep, were taken from the house.

News-Tribune staff photo by Tim Perry

Samuel Tony West

The woman and the other man were taken to a Halls Valley Road residence and released. West and Brock left in the professor's jeep. Two days later West and Brock encountered Kirby Phelps, a 26-year-old naval officer stationed in Jacksonville (FL) at an interstate rest area about 6 or 7 miles east of Vicksburg (MS). The two overpowered

Phelps and walked him to a nearby wooded area where they attempted to handcuff him to a tree. Phelps took a swing at them and West shot him.

Mississippi authorities found Phelps's body the next morning with three .22-caliber gunshot wounds. His body was discovered about 150 feet past the rest area by two men looking for Civil War relics. That rest area is now closed. Mississippi authorities closed it after Phelps was killed.

West and Brock left the rest area, one in the jeep they'd taken from the professor and the other in Phelps' vehicle. They abandoned the professor's black jeep (which was very visible with a white star inside a circle painted on both doors) sometime

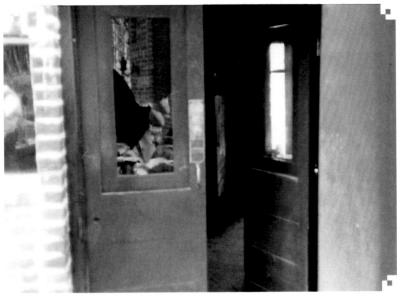

The back door going into the Scudder/Odom home was used most for entry. The glass in the left side of the door had been broken when authorities arrived to investigate the murder of the home owners.

later in Louisiana. From there they continued on in Phelps' Datsun to Texas. In Austin (TX) they got into an argument and split up. Brock came back to Georgia where he was arrested. He had made several calls to family that helped authorities locate him. He was arrested at a service station in Cobb County. West ended up back in Chattanooga (TN) and later gave himself up to Rossville authorities on Christmas morning. At the time of his arrest, West was wearing a silver bracelet inscribed with 'Charles' and was wearing a three-piece brown suit bearing the laundry label 'Phelps.' Neither man

Sheriff Gary McConnell (left) and Chief Investigator Tony Gilleland (right) escort Kenneth Avery Brock to jail as he was arrested for the murders of two Chattooga County residents.

133

ever denied the local killings. West just wasn't as forthcoming as Brock was. I'd say West was more seasoned (as a criminal) than Brock. West was the leader of the two.

The female witness to the local murders, Teresa Hudgins, came forward 12 hours after the killings and provided details that aided in West and Brock's capture.

The trial was held in the county courthouse with Judge Joseph "Bo" Loggins presiding. Loggins was a very thorough, tough, hard-nosed judge. Brock plead guilty and was sentenced to three consecutive life terms in connection with the local murders by Judge Loggins. West was also tried locally before Judge Loggins and was convicted

A view of Corpsewood showing the gazebo and the pink concrete gargoyle on top.

and sentenced to die. However, that sentence was overturned. He was later re-sentenced to life in prison. West pled guilty in Mississippi and was given life in prison without parole and 30 years to run consecutively. Brock pled and received two consecutive life sentences.

This case was unusual in many aspects and there was a lot of speculation that led to the international media attention. Scudder and Odom lived in the middle of 40 acres in the middle of the National Forest. Their house was an odd-shaped oblong, two-story structure that they built by hand. The house was made of brick with air insulation followed by another wall of brick. The men had lived in a small camper on the property while they were constructing the house. It had only two doors, one on the back that you saw when

A 14th Century desk and high back chair in the library of Corpsewoood that murderers ransacked after shooting both residents of the home and their two dogs.

you drove up and one on the front that overlooked where they were building a small pond. There were no regular windows in the house. They used glass blocks in vertical rows on each end to give extra light to the inside of the house and both doors had small windows in the top portions of them.

They had a concrete gargoyle placed on top of their gazebo. The gazebo was attached to the house by a walkway that could be unhinged and removed. There was a three-story outbuilding nearby that housed chickens at one time (bottom floor), their canned goods and supplies (second floor) and a so-called guest room (top floor) that held a mattress and a straight chair and everything in the room was painted pink. The house had no electricity. They used a wood stove to cook on and had a kerosene operated icebox for a refrigerator. Their bathroom was an outside round structure, as was their well house. Inside the house was filled with numerous pieces of antique furniture, skulls and books on the occult. There was talk of homosexuality and drug use at their place. We never had any cause or evidence to warrant us investigating them.

The men were known to be polite when strangers drove up to get a look at their strange house. Lots of rumors circulated in the county because of odd things linked to the place. They called their road Dead Horse Road (a horse carcass had been discarded at the end of the road when they bought the property). They called their property

Corpsewood (they moved onto the property in the winter when all the vegetation was dead and the trees were without leaves). They had a sign just before you got to their yard that read "Beware of The Thing". When most visitors were greeted by one of their dogs they would ask, "What is that thing?" They raised Old English Mastiffs, a breed that had not been seen around here much at that time.

The killings were discovered when one of their

Chief Investigator Tony Gilleland (left) escorts murder suspect Tony Wells West back to jail following a day of trial. Assisting him are Deputies Aubrey Smith and Bert Tucker.

friends hadn't seen them in several days and went to take their mail to them. When he got there, he saw that the glass in the double doors had been shot out. He looked in and saw Odom dead on the floor. He left and called the sheriff's department. Deputies Charlie Starkey and Greg Latta went to investigate. Arriving at the house, they first looked through the glass in the door and saw a body lying on the floor. They secured the scene and notified me. This was around 10:30 a.m.

I had been at a meeting so when I arrived, I had to borrow Greg's 357 magnum before we went

Swamped by reporters as the trial of murder suspect Tony Wells West got underway at the Chattooga County Courthouse. Sheriff Gary McConnell could not answer questions directly about the case due to a gag order imposed by Superior Court Judge Joseph Loggins. The sheriff could only answer questions about his department's compliance with the gag order and tight court security ordered by Judge Loggins.

into the house. As we entered, we found a body lying in the kitchen area that I knew to be Odom. We proceeded from there and saw that both of their dogs had been killed near the stove. Then we discovered Scudder's body lying in the living room area of the house.

There was a concrete spiral staircase that lead to the upper floor where the bedrooms were. There were bloody footprints going up the stairs, but none coming down. Somebody had to go up and it happened to be my job. As you went up the stairs there was a stained-glass window depicting a man gagged with a bullet wound in his head and flies around him.

Once you reached the top of the stairs you just had to stick your head out, there was no way around it. In the larger bedroom, there was a large antique wooden canopy bed with numerous carvings on it. Beside the bed sat a 3 or 4-foot brass-looking devil statue. There was a large gold harp and several skulls, among other things. The other bedroom wasn't as colorful. We found no one else in the house.

There were some unusual items found throughout the house like the skulls and occult-related decorative items. One odd thing I remember was there were about 8 or so eggs in the kitchen in a hutch where they stored their cooking supplies. The eggs were numbered like 5, 9 and such. We never did figure out the significance of that.

It's All About The People

Historical Warren County Courthouse

Photo by Kenneth C. Zirkel

Since there was no electricity in the house, we had to bring in generators to provide light as we searched the house. After searching the house and surrounding buildings thoroughly, we even brought a backhoe in. There had been so many rumors circulating that drugs were being sold there and that they had a lab where they were manufacturing drugs that we had to exhaust every possibility to find the truth. We dug a moat around the house and the bathroom to make sure there were no hidden passages to an underground lab. We had to make sure we weren't missing anything. We never found anything.

Gary W. McConnell

Chattooga County Sheriff Gary McConnell escorting convicted murderer Samuel Tony West back to court in Summerville for a hearing.

It's All About The People

We videotaped the crime scene. It was one of the first times that was done in this part of the state. We borrowed the video camera from a local businessman, Larry Stansell, and Lewis Wilson, a local photographer, videoed the scene.

One of the biggest issues we had to deal with, other than the muddy conditions due to rain, was the sightseers. People were so curious about the men, their property and what had happened. We had to have the traffic stopped on the Narrows Road turned away, as the road coming down to their property was a single lane forestry road. The onlookers got so bad trying to get a chance to get to the scene, GSP set up a roadblock to check licenses. They wrote 30 tickets in one day for people with no license and other violations.

During our investigation, we had to post people on the property for several days to keep sightseers from coming onto the area to see what they could get. People were even trying to take shrubbery out of the yard as a souvenir. Sometime after our investigation was complete, the three-story structure and the house were burned by vandals. The only part of the house that could burn was the roof and the floor of the second story, but some people were determined to destroy what they could of the place.

The case was also in the media's attention because there was a big dispute over the estate. The families of both Odom and Scudder battled in court to see who would receive the property

and the personal effects of the men. The case went back and forth for some time before a judge finally ruled in favor of Scudder's sons. A couple of books and a short film have also been done about the killings.

Had it not been for Ms. Hudgins coming forward about the murders, it would have taken us much longer to have apprehended West and Brock. She called and asked for me. The dispatcher put her on hold and when I answered she said she wanted to talk to me about the killings on the mountain. I went to see her and she told me everything that happened that night.

When I asked her why she had come forward, she said she had talked with her father. He advised her to tell me and that I would treat her fairly (considering she was there during the killings). He said he knew I would because my dad had treated him fairly years before in a situation.

I got the call late Christmas Eve that West had been apprehended in Rossville. I had just finished putting a Big Wheel together for my daughter that Santa was leaving under the tree. I was putting the stickers on it when I had to leave to take custody of West. Diane had to finish getting it ready. West was arrested for the murders by Christmas as I'd said earlier he would be.

In Mississippi, the case against West and Brock wasn't quite as sensational even though it was just as tragic and horrendous. This young sailor was on

his way to Oklahoma to visit his widowed mother for Christmas. They killed him for his vehicle and what they took off him.

During the trial, the handcuffs used on Phelps were lying on the table as evidence. West's lawyer picked up the handcuffs and put them on himself showing how they worked. It was an off brand of handcuffs and none of the law enforcement there had a key that would open them. The judge let the lawyer do about 30 minutes of trial with a handcuff hanging off his wrist. He finally stopped the trial and got the sheriff to get a pair of bolt cutters to cut them off.

Testifying during the first trial in Warren County was a new experience for me. It was the first time my expertise and experience had to be vetted for a jury so that what I testified about was creditable. Testifying in Chattooga, everyone knew my background and law enforcement history. I never had to explain how I knew what I was doing.

One of the things that Warren County D.A. Frank Campbell said when he was arguing to the jury at the close of the case stuck in my mind as a very good statement. West was already convicted of the killings in Chattooga at the time and the jury knew this. They were asking for the death penalty out there. Campbell looked at West and said, "How many is enough? How many do we have to let you kill before we kill you?" I have always remembered that.

Gary W. McConnell

There was an interesting twist to going to Vicksburg for West and Brock's trials. An unusual article was written entitled "A Frightful Murder and Box Supper Years Before" and it was about my mother.

Mother had gone to high school in Mississippi and the guy that wrote the article, Charles Faulk, had dated both my mother and her sister. The article appeared in the Vicksburg Sunday Post on Aug. 23, 1987.

Sometime after the trial, I carried my mother to Vicksburg to visit with two people that she had known in high school. One was the gentleman that wrote the article and the other was a gentleman that owned the Chrysler dealership there in town. It was interesting to see the city from her viewpoint and learn what it was like when she lived there.

When I went to Vicksburg to testify in the West trial, I knew my mother's family had lived there for a time. After the trial I wanted to take her back to the area for a visit. When she called to check on a bed and breakfast in an antebellum home, she talked with Charles Faulk, who turned out to be a former classmate of hers when she attended Jefferson Davis Academy. He went on to write a two-part story about Mother and me that was featured in the Vicksburg (MS) Sunday Post in August of 1987.

The editorial columns covered when mother (the former Marguerite Rea) and her family lived

in the Vicksburg area and my involvement in helping solve the Phelps murder there in 1982.

Mother, her parents (Mr. And Mrs. Bat Rea) and her two sisters (Helen and Gladys), lived in southern Warren County (MS) in the early 1920s. The family had moved to the area from North Georgia. There used to be a big department store in Chattanooga (TN) called Miller Brothers and my mother's dad ran their farming operation for them. The family moved to Vicksburg (MS) and he bought a 3,300-acre plantation there and then the Depression came along. My mother moved back to Chattooga County and the rest of her family moved to Baton Rouge (LA). Her dad went into the trucking business and stayed there until he died of pneumonia. There was a big flood in 1947 and he had a contract to haul dirt to help build the levy over the Mississippi River. He wouldn't let his drivers back his trucks out on the levy because it had gotten so dangerous with all the rain. He backed all the trucks onto the levy working in the rain. He caught pneumonia and died from it.

In the article, Faulk talked about box suppers and how the pretty Rea girls always commanded a premium bid. A box supper is where the girls would prepare fried chicken, side dishes and a dessert at home. The food, enough for two people to eat, was put into an unmarked box or basket and carried to an event. The boxes/baskets would then be raffled off to the highest bidding boy. The boy winning each box would have the privilege of

dining with the girl that prepared that box.

Mother lived in the Vicksburg area for about 10 years before moving to Summerville to work. It was here that she and my dad met and married. She helped with the farm and when Dad became sheriff, she helped there as well. She began working as a substitute rural mail carrier in 1950 and went on to work the last 12 years of her 22-year-career as a full-time carrier before retiring.

Another robbery we investigated occurred in February of 1983 at A.D. Pledger's General Merchandise Store on Highway 27 in the Gore Community. It was a little country store that was owned and operated by an elderly couple in the southern part of the county.

Back then the merchant still put the gasoline in people's cars. Mrs. Addie Lou Pledger, who was working alone that day, put gas in the customers' car. When she went back in the store, she caught one of the robbers stealing money from the cash register. At that point Mrs. Pledger was attacked and beaten with a glass soft drink bottle which broke as she was being beaten. She was also choked. The robbers ransacked the store and fled in their car.

A customer found Mrs. Pledger beaten and notified us. After talking briefly with Mrs. Pledger and several other people in the area, we received enough information to identify one of the robbers. Further investigation led us to identify the other

two involved in the robbery. We arrested all three involved in the robbery and attack within several hours and recovered all the money taken. Mrs. Pledger was treated at a Rome hospital for several days and returned to operating the store with her husband. We arrested Wayne "Fruity" Lavonne Williams, James "Pee Wee" Edward Kirby and Patricia Diane Covington for the robbery.

Before the year was over, we were back in the media's attention when a youngster died at the Campeonada Foundation, a wilderness camp for troubled youths in the Silver Hill Community. The 16-year-old died of suffocation from a severe asthma attack that went untreated. A camp counselor, 31-year-old James Francis Shores, was charged with cruelty to children in connection with the death. The camp was later closed in the county. In addition, a Chattooga County Superior Court Judge later threw out a $3 million libel lawsuit against me in connection with the Campeonada case.

We continued to be vigilant in our efforts to crack down on marijuana growing in the county. With the help of the Governor's Task Force helicopters, we confiscated an estimated $1 million worth of marijuana in a single day's search in the summer of 1983. Within a short time of flying, officers spotted several marijuana patches and fields. Officers on the ground were directed to the marijuana by radios from the officers in the helicopters. We either pulled the plants up by

the roots or cut the stalks off at the ground. The plants were then loaded on vehicles and taken to a local textile plant where they were burned in their furnace.

Meanwhile, the problem with the county jail being overcrowded continued and in early 1983 the county was ordered by a federal judge to correct the problem. We held several public meetings with the residents of the county to determine how they wanted to pay for the jail project. A bond referendum was passed by the voters in Chattooga a short time later and the renovation of adding

A crowd of 800 to 1,000 attended the Open House for the new Chattooga County Jail. The 47-inmate capacity facility was funded by a $925,000 bond issue approved by county voters in 1983. Outgoing County Commissioner Wayne "Pete" Denson (left) and Sheriff Gary McConnell congratulate each other on the near completion of the project.

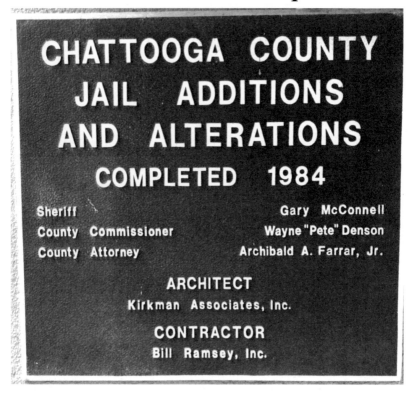

CHATTOOGA COUNTY
JAIL ADDITIONS
AND ALTERATIONS
COMPLETED 1984

Sheriff Gary McConnell
County Commissioner Wayne "Pete" Denson
County Attorney Archibald A. Farrar, Jr.

ARCHITECT
Kirkman Associates, Inc.

CONTRACTOR
Bill Ramsey, Inc.

onto the existing jail began.

Good and bad news on the issue of housing prisoners in the county continued. By January of 1985 the new jail construction was finished but heating problems caused a delay in being able to house prisoners in it. During the same time, Georgia Gov. Joe Frank Harris signed a bill approving funds for the new state prison to be built in the Pennville Community.

We were able to correct the heating problems and soon began housing prisoners in our new county facility. Despite the problems we had getting into the new jail, we went on to be one of only 15 county jails in the state to be certified

by the Georgia Chapter of the American Medical Association. The medical association awards the certificate for the high medical and health care standards at a jail facility.

Receiving the accreditation on the first try was nearly impossible and most jails don't achieve it right off. We received it and continued to receive it year after year thanks to the wonderful work of Dr. Herman Spivey. Dr. Spivey wrote the medical care protocols for the jail and maintained an excellent quality of care program for the jail.

With the opening of the new county jail, I wanted the residents to understand that restrictions and regulations had to be followed under the federal court order. Forming the Sheriff's Advisory Board was a way for citizens to have a better understanding of the department's operations from people they knew and trusted. The board members were comprised of local residents and business leaders throughout the county. They asked questions and reported back to the citizens. Board members were surprised and dismayed at the cost involved in complying with the court order. The non-political advisory committee was one of only two in the state at that time.

In the day-to-day activities of a sheriff you never think about yourself being kidnapped. But I learned in March of 1984 that it can happen, especially if it's for a worthy cause. The Oak View Nursing Home was raising funds for the American Heart Association through various activities. One

of their fund-raising projects was to "kidnap" local residents and hold them for ransom. They decided to "kidnap" me and held me for a couple of hours before Walker County Sheriff Ralph Jones brought in a sizable contribution as my ransom fee.

During the Georgia Sheriff's Association (GSA) annual convention that year (1983), we presented Ms. Hudgins a Meritorious Service Award for coming forward concerning the murders of Charles Scudder and Joey Odom. I was also honored with the 1983 Sheriff of the Year award for my efforts in law enforcement and work with neglected, needy and abandoned children throughout the state. In addition, I was elected second vice-president of the GSA.

I was elected President of the Georgia Sheriffs' Association serving for the 1985-86 term. The following is a reprint of the message I shared with members of the GSA in our Fall 1985 magazine.

Let's look at the future – What will happen?

What is going to be? I don't want to attempt to foretell the future, but there are many things that I would like for the Georgia Sheriffs' Association to accomplish during my term as President.

The most basic accomplishment and one that is already very effective in our association is the cooperation of the sheriffs to promote good law enforcement

Gary W. McConnell

Sheriff Gary McConnell presents Chattooga resident Teresa Hudgins with a Meritorious Service Award for coming forward with information in the murders of Charles Scudder and Joey Odom. The award was presented during the annual Georgia Sheriff's Association convention in Callaway Gardens in 1983.

Photo courtesy of The Summerville News

for the people of Georgia. As an association of 159 sheriffs, we are constantly working to improve legislation, training, and community service.

The future of our Youth Homes continues to look bright. The Sheriffs of Georgia owe the success of this program to you, our honorary members. By offering your helping hand we have been able to change the future of many of our state's children. Let us continue to reduce juvenile delinquency and take good care of these neglected children.

During my term as President, there are some things I do want to make happen. The first is the improvement of the sheriff's image. Because of the downfall of a few lawmen our whole group has been penalized.

I feel that it is very important that we start now to prove to the citizens of Georgia and, most important, our friends and honorary members that have stood beside us, that the sheriffs are dedicated and professional lawmen.

Each day we have to face a criminal element that continues to work against us and any rewards are few and far between. But, as the representatives of a strong and dedicated association of Georgia sheriffs,

Gary W. McConnell

we will continue to give the best protection possible.

An important step in improving law enforcement is to look at the salaries that we pay our local officers. The Sheriffs' Association this year will take up legislatively the issue of peace officer pay.

Statistics show that Georgia pays its officers over $6,000 below the national average. We also rank sixth out of the six Southeastern states.

GSA President Gary W. McConnell (left) presenting 20-year plaques to Faye Carter and James 'Bud' Cody for their dedicated service to the Georgia Sheriff's Association and the Georgia Sheriff's Association Youth Homes.

It's All About The People

Statewide the average pay for an entry-level peace officer in Georgia is $10,842. This figure is only $192 above the state poverty level for a family of four.

It is important that our Youth Homes supporters and our Association supporters look with us at the salaries we pay the men and women out on the street that are protecting our families from the criminal element. We will need your active support during the 1986 legislative session.

In closing, I would like to thank all of my fellow sheriffs for the opportunity to serve as President of our Association. It is truly an honor for me as we individually and as an association continue to take the lead in fighting crime and protecting our citizens.

Tony Gilleland was my chief investigator for several years. He was a good investigator, but we had a disagreement over a policy issue. I fired him in October of 1985 for what I felt was misusing evidence in a felony case. In December of 1985 Tony filed a $1.5-million lawsuit against me saying he had been dismissed without justification. The lawsuit went back and forth in the court system and was tried in mid-June of 1987 but ended in a mistrial when the six-member jury was hopelessly deadlocked. The case was rescheduled for trial, but in August of 1987 the lawyers reached a settlement. It was agreed upon and sealed so nothing else needs to be or can be said about that.

Throughout the years of my administration, we've had a number of bank robberies. Thankfully, no one was ever seriously injured and we were able to apprehend those involved. In fact, the bank in Menlo was once robbed by a couple of guys from Sand Mountain who were on their way to Ringgold to be tried for armed robbery there!

Long before you heard about bombs being left in public places, we had one left at a local bank - or so it seemed. We got a call that a live explosive device had been found in the First National Bank of Chattooga County. This was in October of 1986. When we got to the bank, located on Commerce Street in Summerville, we found the device on the desk of the bank president, Sue Hurley.

After talking with Mrs. Hurley about the device and about who could have possibly left it, I gingerly took it outside and tossed it over a fence into a vacant lot. The bomb squad from Fort Gillem came up. The device wasn't a live bomb. It was just four truck flares taped together to look like dynamite. No one was ever arrested for the stunt, but we figured it was probably left by a patron that was upset over his dealings with the bank.

When living in a fairly small community all of your life and also serving the public, investigating crimes can be a bit more difficult at times. You always have to stay focused on the job at hand and not let your emotions show or affect you at that time. This has been especially hard for me numerous times, but there are two separate

occasions that still remain with me to this day. The first was in 1974 and the second was in 1987.

One of the best friends I ever had was Peter Boney. Peter and I went through high school together and played football together. When I became sheriff, he would spend a lot of time at the sheriff's department with me. The day of his accident, he spent all day with me.

It was close to his birthday in 1974. Later on that night, a member of his family called me and said they couldn't find him. We searched and located him close to his backyard dead from a single gunshot wound. He was living just off Farrar Drive at the time. It was hard to pick him up and go tell his parents and his kids what had happened. Sadly, that was my job.

I knew him as well as I knew anybody in my life. I spent approximately six hours with him that day and we were talking about stuff we were going to do the next week. We both had cattle at the time and were talking about maybe going to a cattle sale and buying some cows.

A case in August of 1987 had a profound effect on me. Two elderly sisters were brutally attacked in their home in the Chattoogaville Community and left for dead. We found Miss Lorraine Elrod, 71, badly injured and she had to be hospitalized for some time. Her 75-year-old sister, Miss Gertie Estelle Elrod, had died from her injuries before we found her. The ladies had been tied together with

a cord from a lamp and left on a bed.

I played Santa Claus every year at the Sardis Baptist Church the sisters attended next door to their home. They always allowed me to change into my Santa suit and wait in their home so the kids wouldn't see me beforehand. They were very sweet ladies who were always willing to help anyone in need (including their attacker). They never bothered anyone or caused a moment's problem.

The brutality against them caused my emotions to surface despite my years of training and experience dealing with homicides. I wanted

EMTs put Miss Lorraine Elrod in an ambulance to be taken to the hospital after being severely beaten and left for dead.

Photo from The Summerville News by Tommy Toles

immediate justice that day. I didn't get it in the way I wanted at the time, but we did get justice for them in the days that followed and it was in the way it should have been.

Mrs. Lillian Drummond, another sister, had gone to the Elrod home on that Friday morning (Aug. 28) to spend the day with her sisters. When she found the back door open and she couldn't find her sisters, she went to a neighbor's and asked for help. The neighbor returned to the Elrod home with Mrs. Drummond. When he broke a bedroom door open, they discovered the sisters tied up and lying side-by-side on a bed. Both women had been beaten about the head with an electric iron.

When we arrived at the scene, we found Miss Gertie was dead and Miss Lorraine was in critical condition. We estimated the sisters had been lying on the bed for about 15 hours. When I picked Miss Lorraine up and put her on the stretcher, she gave me a very accurate and complete description of the person who had attacked them. The murderer was Jonathan Jarrells, a 30-year-old West Virginian who had been staying with relatives across the road from the Elrods.

He had arrived in the county on Sunday (Aug. 23). In fact, the sisters had let him obtain water from their home earlier in the week prior to the attack. The house he had been staying in has since been torn down.

The brutality of Jarrells' actions made me so

mad I wanted to kill him. We were going across the street to the house where we thought he might be. I told Deputy Greg Latta (who was going to the back door of the residence), "If I don't come out the door first, shoot whoever does." I wanted him (Jarrells) dead. It dawned on me that day I needed to think about possibly doing something else for a living. I didn't need to be the one catching him, trying him and executing him in the backyard of the home he had been staying in. That's what I wanted to do that day. Justice prevailed and the right thing happened. That was one of the few times I thought I should just kill him right then. The incident made me do a little personal examining and wondering if I could do the job of sheriff the best way I knew how.

A lookout was placed for Jarrells based on Miss Lorraine's information. We had a GSP helicopter come up and help us search the wooded area for Jarrells. While they were flying, they discovered a patch of marijuana in the Chattoogaville area. That was just a reminder that other aspects of law enforcement don't stop just because you have a murderer you're searching for.

After we talked to Jarrells' relatives, we put a nationwide lookout for him and the 1984 Mazda he was driving. We determined that he was probably heading back home to West Virginia or Kentucky where he had been working. Slightly more than eight hours after the sisters were found, a suspect fitting Jarrells' description and driving a

It's All About The People

Mazda was spotted by a toll booth operator on the Daniel Boone Parkway. The operator notified the Kentucky State Police and Jarrells was stopped about six miles from the toll booth. We later learned that Jarrells was at a local car wash on the Lyerly Highway washing his truck Friday morning. He saw all the emergency and law enforcement vehicles headed to the Chattoogaville area before he left town that day.

Jarrells was from Mingo County, West Virginia. Deputy Greg Latta and I went up there prior to his trial seeking any information we could get. That's the poorest place I've ever been to in my

Chattooga Chief Investigator Ron Turner (left to right) and Chattooga Sheriff Gary McConnell escort Jonathan Jarrells into the Chattooga County Jail after he was found in Hazard, Kentucky, on his way to Mingo County, West Virginia, and returned to Chattooga for the murder of Miss Gertie Elrod and the attempted murder of her sister, Miss Lorraine Elrod.

life. There's poverty everywhere. The day before I got there the federal government had arrested 38 local officials for corruption, pretty much the whole elected structure of Mingo County. Trying

Murderer Jonathan Jarrells escorted by Sheriff Gary McConnell

to find out anything, being from Georgia and not knowing anyone, was a little bit difficult. I knew the names of the people I was looking for and I finally found someone at the post office who told me how to find them.

Jonathan Jarrells

There was one family in particular I needed to talk to. They lived up this little road next to a river and it was winter time when we went up there. When Greg and I got to the house, it was a little three room shack with tar paper around it. It was snowing and there were no windows in the house. They just had sheets covering the openings. It had a plank going up to one of the windows so the chickens could go in the house. We went in and were talking to them. There are chickens in the house and this little boy came riding through on a skateboard. He was down on his knees sort of. He had polio and the only way he could get around was on that skateboard.

They were some of the nicest people you'd ever want to talk to. They were just really, really poor. They had some information we needed and I asked him if he'd come to Georgia and testify. The fellow

said, "Sheriff I'd love to but I haven't any gas and I don't have any money." I pulled four $100 bills out of my pocket and gave to him. I said, "This will get you down there and we'll get you a place to stay when you get there." It was like he'd never seen that much money at one time before in his life. He and his family came down here and we interviewed him again. He testified to the living conditions Jarrells grew up in in Mingo County. He didn't have any direct testimony about the murders since he wasn't here.

I've seen a lot of poverty in my life, just like everyone has, but that was the worst. I'll never forget that kid on that skateboard. Mingo County is the poorest county in the United States. It's in the middle of the Appalachian coal mining area of West Virginia.

Sometimes it takes a funny incident in a case to help keep things in perspective and get you through it. We were going to Hazard, KY, to pick up Jarrells for the Elrod killing. It was me, a GBI agent, a deputy, and a court reporter. As I mentioned, the Daniel Boone Parkway was a toll road. I got to the toll booth, flipped out my diamond badge and showed it to the lady. I don't even know why I had that badge with me. She commented generally, "That's very nice and I'm sure it means a lot in Georgia but it'll be a dollar and a half, sheriff." I told her we were on our way to Hazard to pick up a suspect wanted for murder in Georgia. She said she knew about that case because she was the one

who spotted the suspect and called the Kentucky State Police. So, I put the badge back in my pocket and gave the lady a dollar and a half and we went on our way. She was a very nice lady just doing her job. You had to laugh and not get mad at her. I was glad she was so observant.

The trial for Jarrells was moved to Walker County because of all the news coverage it had received locally. I was worried that Miss Lorraine might not be able to identify Jarrells as her attacker with all the trauma she had endured. She had been hospitalized for some time and was in a wheelchair. When she was called as a witness, I rolled her into the courtroom in her wheelchair. She punched me on the hand and I leaned over to see what she needed. She quietly said, "That's him right there" and clearly knew who had attacked her.

Over the years we were fortunate not to have a lot of problems at the jail. However, there was an unusual incident that happened there and involved the only time a weapon was discharged in the facility. I had brought in a prisoner on some charge and was processing him into the system when Deputy Johnny Bass anxiously approached me saying he needed to talk to me. I told him I'd talk to him later, but he insisted he needed to talk right then. I asked him what was wrong and he said, "I shot the adding machine." Sure enough, looking around there were pieces of the machine everywhere. I asked him what had the adding

machine done wrong? The deputy, who is an avid gun collector, said he was cleaning his service weapon and somehow it discharged striking the adding machine. I advised him to keep his gun in his holster from then on, especially when he was in the office.

Talking about discharging firearms, I never shot anyone but was shot at twice as was noted earlier. I have shot up in the air trying to get them to stop (they just ran faster). The only time I had a deputy to shoot anyone involved a young man on Orchard Road trying to commit suicide. The boy was threatening his family and to commit suicide. Jadie Price, my Chief Deputy, had been a sniper in the Vietnam War and I asked him if he could shoot the boy without fatally wounding him. He shot him in the wrist and made him drop the knife he was threatening with. We were able to get the family away from him, arrested him and got treatment for his wound.

Not having to discharge our firearms any more than we did during my tenure as sheriff probably couldn't be accomplished today for several reasons. You have a different type criminal today, especially drug-related. They are more violence prone. Law enforcement is more on edge and rightfully so. We live in a very uneasy time worldwide now.

Thinking back on some of the murder cases I've dealt with, there is one criminal that stands out. Of all the criminals I dealt with involving cases that resulted in death penalty cases, one person

was the hard-hardest, coldest and seemed to be the most vicious of all those defendants: Judith Ann Neelley.

If you looked into her eyes or when she looked at you, she looked like she could just stare a hole through you. Her demeanor and attitude was much harder than Whisman, Chatterton, Jarrells and such. Judith Ann Neelley was cold hearted, had no regret, and apparently did not respect life in any form.

She was callous and manipulating. Look at the crimes they committed, especially what they did to the young girl in DeKalb County (injected her with Drano, shot her and then pushed her off a cliff into the Little River Canyon). It was just brutal. Yes, what Chatterton, Whisman, Jarrells, and the others did was also brutal, especially Jarrells with the older women, but Judith went to the extremes. She was smart, cute, cruel and she used all of that to her advantage. She was very controlling. She was by far the driving force of the couple.

Gary W. McConnell

More photos from inside Corpsewood

Close-up of the stained glass window overlooking the staircase.

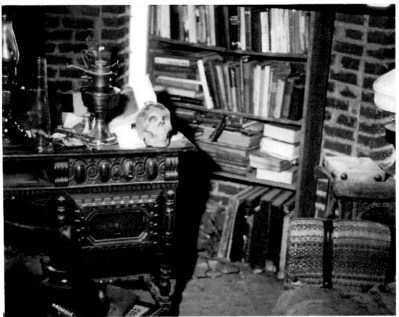

A skull sat on the desk inside Corpsewood (above). The bookshelf was packed with an assortment of genres from the occult to botanical gardening. The antique desk (below) in the home of Dr. Charles Scudder and Joey Odom.

A mirror hanging inside Corpsewood (above). A concrete gargoyle (below), which the owners had painted pink, sat atop the gazebo attached to Corpsewood.

It's All About The People

The windows in Corpsewood (left) were made out of either blocks of glass or stained glass.

An unique statue (right) sat on the nightstand upstairs next to Dr. Charles Scudder's bed.

Scenes from inside Corpsewood

There were no corners throughout the home as it was built in an oblong shape, as were the rooms inside. There was also no electricity or running water in the house. A small circle building at the back of the house served as a well house.

Gary W. McConnell

The house was heated by a wood heater. Kerosene lamps and candles were used for lights in the home.

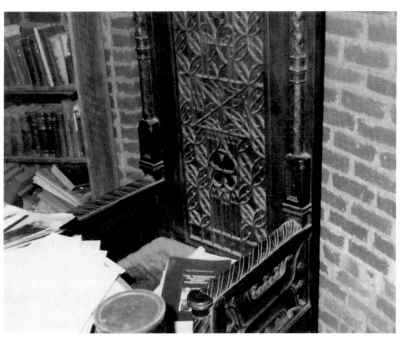

17
Serving the County

We conducted a massive drug raid in March of 1988 that resulted in three people being arrested, and the seizure of cocaine and marijuana, along with almost $60,000 in cash and a number of vehicles. We arrested a Summerville man and his mother, along with another local woman. This was the second time we'd arrested the man on drug charges in less than a year. In fact, he hadn't been tried on the first charges when we made the

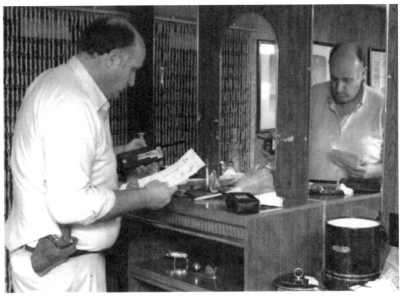

Sheriff Gary McConnell is shown searching the home of a Summerville man relating to a massive drug raid. Authorities seized suspected drugs and drug-related items throughout the house.

second group of charges.

We had seized about $73,000 in the first arrest. During the second arrest, we found $59,614.85 in cash and seized seven vehicles and one trailer designed to haul vehicles valued at more than $50,000. The cars were a 1976 black Dodge Charger, 1968 red-orange Plymouth Road Runner, a 1970 red Plymouth Barracuda, and others.

One thing I found sad about the whole situation was that the man's father had died several months earlier. While we were searching the residence, we found a bill from one of the local funeral homes for the burial. With all the money on hand, nothing had been paid on his father's funeral bill.

You're always hearing about bad cops, cops that are corrupt and on the take. Well, I had the opportunity to work with a cop that exemplified the highest standards of law enforcement. Ron Turner, who was my chief investigator at the time, was one honest cop. He was approached by two local brothers offering him bribes in connection with their drug business and he came directly to me about the situation.

It all began when we conducted a drug raid at the residence of Ronald "Danny Boy" Adams in Summerville in early March of 1988. We had received complaints from neighbors in the area of suspected drug activity at the Adams house. We searched the residence and didn't find any drugs, but several thousand dollars in cash. Since there

were no drugs in the house, we couldn't confiscate the money.

We continued to patrol the area in connection with the complaints. Ron was on patrol one afternoon when the Adams brothers (Danny Boy and his younger brother, William 'Little Bill') stopped him. After some small talk, Danny Boy told Ron there was a lot of money to be made in his (Adams') line of business and he (Ron) had hurt his operation. Ron asked them if they had a tape recorder with them trying to set him up. They said that wasn't how they worked. In fact, they told him that the big money could be split three ways and include him. Ron told them there were too many people that could see them talking and he needed time to think about it. He left them and came straight to me and told me what had happened. We contacted the GBI and filled them in on the situation.

They approached Ron the next day while he was off duty. He asked how much money they were talking about and what they wanted from him. They said $50,000 to $60,000 could be made selling cocaine. Ron told them that since he was in law enforcement, he could only provide them with information about upcoming drug raids. They said they'd pay $300 to $400 a week for that kind of information. A few days later they approached him again and said they'd pay him $1,000 a week. Since he was in a patrol car, he told them he'd meet them that night. He came to me and we set

up electronic surveillance for the meeting. They met and he was given $1,000 in cash. He returned to the sheriff's department and we put the money in an evidence bag. He met with them four more times. Each time we had electronic surveillance covering the meeting. He was given $2,800 on the next meeting, then $1,200 and $1,000 at the last two meetings. In addition, he was given two grams of cocaine.

After a three-week operation, we decided to conclude it with a raid at Danny Boy's residence. We called in the GBI and the FBI to assist us. When we got to the house to serve the search warrant, no one answered so I kicked in the front door.

Chattooga County Investigator Ron Turner (left) and Sheriff Gary McConnell shown with suspected cocaine and marijuana scales found in a house searched as part of the investigation into the Adams Brothers incident.

It's All About The People

After a search of the residence, we seized more than five ounces of cocaine, more than a pound of high quality marijuana, five vehicles, slightly more than $100 in cash, a list of suspected drug users, scales, and a large quantity of furniture and electronic equipment. We also found two beepers, one in Danny Boys' sports car and one on him. The beepers were used by Ron to contact Danny Boy and we had a record of each time they were used. The drugs were turned over to the GBI for analysis at the state crime lab.

Both brothers were charged with nine counts of

I gave a drug talk at the Oak Hill Baptist Church in the Gore Community where I talked about the dangers of various drugs available to youngsters in the county. I explained that marijuana wasn't the only dangerous drug that youngsters were experimenting with. I told them that drugs, including medicine taken from the family medicine cabinet and swapped with friends, as well as alcohol, were a threat to youngsters.

bribery, delivering cocaine, trafficking in cocaine, and violating the Georgia Controlled Substances Act for possessing almost two pounds of marijuana. Danny Boy was also charged with being a convicted felon in the possession of a firearm.

We see a lot of drugs and money out there and it's tempting to some lawmen to turn their heads the other way. This proved that a lot of folks took their responsibilities seriously and that they would not yield to the temptation of easy money. As I said, Ron was one honest cop.

In law enforcement, you are constantly dealing with heated situations and have to know how to handle them in a manner that solves the problem without getting out of control. William "Little Bill" Adams, who had a reputation for supposedly being pretty bad to deal with, showed up again later in a tense situation. He had been acquitted on the charging of bribing Turner, while his brother was sentenced to a total of 135 years in prison.

Large crowd disperses after arrival of Sheriff McConnell

It's All About The People

Deputies were attempting to serve warrants on Adams in connection with an earlier domestic dispute when he fled on foot. He was caught a short time later and as officers attempted to put him in a patrol car, a crowd began to gather. Officers called for additional assistance

A handcuff had been placed on one of his wrists, but because of his strength, officers couldn't get the other cuff on him. A struggle ensued as Adams fought with officers resisting arrest. The crowd was continuing to gather when I arrived. When I approached, the crowd began to move back. I'd always had a pretty good relationship with the black community. Someone from the local paper said the sheriff got there and it was like the parting of the sea. The group had been gathered around the police car and they just stepped back.

I told Adams he would have to get in the patrol car and he did. It wasn't out of fear for me, it was just out of respect because I'd always gotten along with the black community and treated them right and with respect.

Sometimes in your life things come full circle if you wait long enough. In the August 1988 election, I was challenged by the man that my dad had defeated to become sheriff that started me on this path. Former sheriff Fred Stewart was my only challenger in that election. I won the election with 77 percent of the votes and carried all 13 precincts. I received 4,574 votes while Stewart received 1,386 votes.

18
My Fourth Term as Sheriff

Being sheriff wasn't always about investigating crimes and arresting people. In September of 1988 the county hosted the re-enactment of the 125th anniversary of the Battle of Chickamauga. The event was held on the old Underwood Dairy and Selman property in the Pennville Community that had just been purchased for the building of the state prison. Temporary roads had been built into the property, but construction on the prison itself hadn't begun. It was the ideal spot. The entrance was off U.S. Highway 27 and there were plenty of open fields for the reenactors to conduct their battles. The merchants had an area to set up and there was room for those camping, and plenty of room for spectators.

With an event of that size we had to deal with a lot going on behind the scenes. We had to provide security for the event, we had to deal with traffic control, you had to deal with any minor (or major) disagreements that might occur between the reenactors, the spectators, and then between the two groups. These issues weren't just during the hours the event was open to the public. We also had to deal with problems throughout the night.

It's All About The People

To make matters worse, we had some heavy rains during the event weekend. Some of the reenactors had camped across the river on the Klatt property and had to be rescued because of flooding. I called in W.A. and Mike Hutchins with their farm tractors and cotton wagons to carry everyone out because the river was rising so quickly. A couple of small walking bridges had been built across the river for the campers. We had to tear those up because they were holding debris and causing even more flooding. All and all, it went well and we didn't have any major injuries.

Gov. Lester Maddox came to Chattooga quite a bit before and during his term as governor of Georgia. His brother-in-law lived on the mountain (Cloudland). He also hired a lady from here (Carolyn Webster from Menlo) to work in his administration. I had some dealings with him when he was governor because of his connections to Chattooga.

The last time I saw him alive was at the governor's mansion. He was sort of a character. We were having something for Gov. (Joe Frank) Harris, a birthday party or something. I didn't know Gov. Maddox was anywhere around. Somebody behind me ran and jumped upon my back like a kid would pretending to ride your back like a horse. It was Gov. Lester Maddox. That was just him (Maddox). Lester made a lot of good appointments while he was governor. He was a little controversial as a governor, but surrounded himself with many smart

people. A couple of those were Tommy Irvin and Zell Miller. He was instrumental in getting them started on their careers or helped their careers.

I was elected president of the 800-member County Officials Association of Georgia (C.O.A.G.) in 1989. The C.O.A.G. is composed of local constitutional officers in Georgia, excluding county commissioners. The group represents clerks of court, probate judges, coroners, sheriffs, and tax commissioners. C.O.A.G. reviews all legislation affecting local governments with an eye toward maintaining local control of government. All local elected officials are interested in making sure that their posts remain elective and not be made into appointive positions by the state. The people should maintain control over their local business by electing their local officials and not have them taken over by some state master plan.

Another tense situation involved members of the Ku Klux Klan (KKK) and a couple of rallies they held in Summerville and Lyerly on Saturday, May 13, 1989. Thankfully, both events were uneventful without very much disturbance. The first rally was held in downtown Summerville at the courthouse. It not only involved members of the KKK (men, women, and children), some dressed in robes, but it also involved Skinheads. Members of both groups filled the streets, along with residents of the county wanting to see what was going on. We blocked off part of a side street so traffic could continue to flow through town in

front of the courthouse.

After the rally, Don Romine, the grand dragon of the Klan walked to Summerville City Hall and accepted a summons for allegedly violating the city's public address (PA) system ordinance. The council had refused to issue the Klan a permit for the rally but Romine had agreed in advance to accept the summons after the rally. It was a peaceful process. In fact, there were only two arrests made during the afternoon rally and they weren't directly connected to the event. Two local

Scene from the Ku Klux Klan rally in downtown Summerville as speakers stand on the steps of the county courthouse.

Photo courtesy of The Summerville News

residents were arrested in connection with public drunkenness near the second rally site in Lyerly.

I got a lot of state help with both rallies. It was

obvious that I was going to the state if (Zell) Miller won (the governorship). We had the Skinheads and the Klan at the rally at the courthouse. They got together as close as I am thick, literally. I had one at my back and one at my chest.

At the Lyerly rally we had some 300 tactical squad guys here for that one. There was a big crowd. We had the Klan members in a

Summerville Police Chief Arlen Thomas and Sheriff Gary McConnell oversee the crowd gathering for the KKK rally in downtown Summerville.

Photo courtesy of The Summerville News

yard and then a group of African-Americans on a nearby hill. They were constantly yelling back and forth and doing things to upset each other like blowing an air horn so you couldn't hear yourself think. At one point a PA system was set up by the African-Americans who entertained the Klan with singing and a sermon. A state helicopter circled the Lyerly site several times during the event serving as an aerial observation post.

The Lyerly rally went on for hours. Finally, we asked how long before they were going to burn their cross and conclude their rally. They said it was going to be awhile. We told them we were tired

Sheriff Gary McConnell (second from left) talks with Lyerly residents during a KKK rally at a residential home in the area. GBI Agent Claude Nix (left) was part of the security detail.

Photo courtesy of The Summerville News

and we were leaving soon so both crowds would have to deal with each other on their own. They decided it was time to burn the cross and wrap up their rally. Thankfully, there were no major problems that day with either rally.

Over the years I was involved in many fundraisers for everything from the Subligna Gym to the Lyerly Recreation Department to the Shriners to whatever you want to name. At the Shriners' events they always had a pie contest where they would put a pie in your face. One year a gentleman brought his own pie with him that he had made and put red pepper in it. The pepper nearly choked me and got in my eyes. In the

Sheriff Gary McConnell (No. 39) and Phil Cagle are shown soaring up to tip-off the basketball game between the Summerville-Trion Optimist Club and the Chattooga County officials. The event was a fundraiser for the Lyerly Recreation Department.

189

Playing Santa Claus each year for the annual Christmas parade and for various churches and organizations was one of the fun aspects of being sheriff.

coming years, we continued doing the pie in the face, but the Shriners began furnishing the pies.

When Zell Miller was running for governor of Georgia in 1989, attorney Bobby Lee Cook Sr. and I co-sponsored a big barbecue event for him at the Silver Leaf Resort in the Silver Hill Community. There was a good turnout of about 300 residents.

Zell got good support out of Chattooga County and the residents of Chattooga County received good support from him when he became governor.

During his campaign, Zell and his wife, Shirley, took a group of people to New York City and asked me to be their security. We had been to a Broadway play and were returning to our hotel one evening. Zell, Shirley and I were in the front of the group walking. The Millers stepped off the curb into the street just as a horse-drawn tour carriage came around and almost hit Shirley. I reached up and grabbed the horse's reins, stopped it and let everyone cross the street. Somehow that action made the Atlanta Journal and an edition of the Georgia Beat.

When we were building the state prison, Dave Evans (head of the Department of Corrections) came up here to see the neighborhood and wanted to visit Howard Finster. During the visit, Preacher Finster got to talking to him about Vienna Sausage. Finster loved Vienna Sausage. He said, "Sheriff, I can go down to Hurley's (a local grocery store) and buy a six-pack of Vienna Sausage for 99 cents. I pull them little tops off, paint something on them and sell those things for $10 apiece. I can get $60 for six cans of Vienna Sausage, make $59 and still get to eat the Vienna Sausage."

To show you how the rescue squads have improved over the years, I remember we had a wreck on the top of Taylor's Ridge. There's a big embankment there going down on the right. A car

It's All About The People

went down it. This was back when I had just become sheriff. Somebody was way down the embankment and there wasn't any other way to get them out. We got down there, put them on a stretcher and it was real steep coming back out. I remember we took a rope and tied it to the stretcher and tied the other end around my waist. I got down on my hands and knees and crawled back up the embankment with it. There were some other folks helping push it but I had the rope tied around me like a mule pulling it up the bank. Times have changed. Now people want a piece of equipment to do everything. If you have the equipment, it's good to use but if you don't have it, you've got to do it anyway.

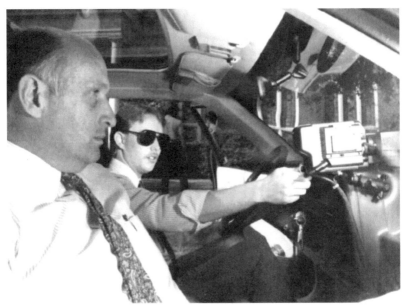

Putting cameras in our patrol cars early was one way to help deputies in the daily performance of their jobs to serve and protect the residents of Chattooga County. Sheriff Gary McConnell (left) is shown with a representative from the camera equipment company.

Gary W. McConnell

We were part of a $60,000 pilot project conducted by a national computer software company in August of 1989. The project didn't cost us anything. The only condition was that the firm was allowed to display the equipment and program to other interested law agencies around the state for one to two years.

We were fortunate to get the pilot project as it wasn't offered to any other sheriff's department in the state. We were able to obtain the project due to my stature as president of the County Officials Association of Georgia and my long-time service as sheriff. We had to pay for several staff members to be trained to use the equipment. We were able to pay for the training with money confiscated from drug dealers so it didn't cost the taxpayers anything either. The system was the most sophisticated law enforcement tool in use north of Atlanta at that time for jail and record management.

A team from the computer company was in the county for several months to help put the five-station networking system in operation after it was installed. The software included databases for jail management and records management, It integrated mapping and crime point analysis. Using a county map, we were able to plot the location of all crimes and determine if one area was being hit harder by a certain crime than other areas. The system also served the county volunteer fire departments which were dispatched from the sheriff's department at that time. It helped

locate the nearest fire department when a fire was reported.

Being involved in the Sheriffs Association helped our county in a number of ways. We put cameras in our patrol cars early on when they were just beginning to start putting them in cars in other areas of the state. Getting the cameras was kind of a result of my being involved in the Sheriffs Association and seeing what they were doing in the metro counties. It showed how well it was working not only to protect the officers, but to protect the defendants and provide factual evidence in court. It was good for the defense and the prosecution and it was meant to give the officers a sense of security. The cameras are just another example of how being involved outside the community benefited the county. I was exposed to them in other places and was able to bring them to our county. At the time, we outfitted both of our patrol cars with the cameras. When I later left office, all eight of the marked patrol cars were equipped with cameras.

We were also one of the first counties in Northwest Georgia to put in an intoximeter when they first came out for the prosecution of DUI (driving under the influence) cases. Over the years we were able to advance the county's ability to provide better public safety. When we first went into office there was a radio in the jail and one portable radio to use in the car when we finally got one. Later on, we were able to get a new low band

system and put them in the cars. Then the state changed and went to a high band radio system for better coverage and more accurate coverage. That's when we installed a tower on Taylor's Ridge where it's still located today. The sheriff's office and the county installed the tower. It was the first time we had complete coverage of the county on a two-way radio system.

Sometimes Mother Nature throws you a curve ball and different things to deal with other than just crime and catching criminals. We were faced with a natural disaster in February of 1990 when torrential rain caused extreme flooding throughout the county, especially hitting the Trion area hard. One resident died locally and another died in a neighboring Alabama county due to the massive flooding.

Flood water started rising quickly and areas were becoming impassable. At the time, there were two-story apartments along Park Avenue in Trion. Due to the Chattooga River being close by, residents were notified to evacuate. I started organizing the evacuation and the water kept rising. We were having to use a back hoe to travel down the street checking to make sure everyone had gotten out.

I can't swim so I had a rope tied to me and the other end tied to the back hoe just in case something happened. I was riding in the bucket of the back hoe as we went down the street. We got to an apartment at the far end of Park Avenue

It's All About The People

An aerial photo of how the Trion City Schools and surrounding businesses and homes looked during the 1990 flood.

Sheriff Gary McConnell being interviewed by a Channel 9 newsman out of Chattanooga (TN) about the 1990 flood.

Photo courtesy of The Summerville News

Trion Elementary School ruined by raging flood waters.

Photo courtesy of The Summerville News

Trion Church of Christ ravaged by the 1990 flood waters.

Photo courtesy of The Summerville News

nearest the river. The water was already about three-feet-deep in the first floor of the apartment.

There was an elderly lady standing on the stairs going to her second floor and refusing to leave her house. I told her, "Ma'am you need to leave." She asked me who I was and I told her, then she asked me who my grandfather was. I told her who he was. She thought a minute and then said she'd go with me because my grandfather had helped her family during the war so she trusted me. I truly believe that lady would not have gone with me had she not known my grandfather.

At one point, the flood was so bad we thought the Trion Dam had burst but it hadn't. Water was coming over the top of it so fast that it appeared it had. The flood did so much damage throughout

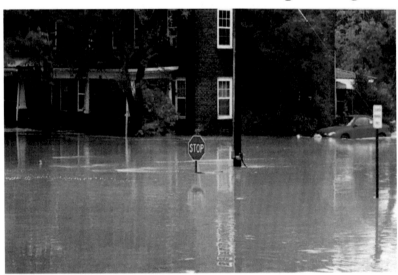

The Park Avenue Apartments in Trion were quickly flooding and the only way to reach the residents still in their homes was by riding in the bucket of a back hoe.

the entire county, but the Trion area was hardest hit. Trion Town Hall was flooded even though it had been built above the floodplain. Riegel Textile (now known as Mount Vernon Mills) was also shut down for several days due to flooding in their plant causing some damage. Both the high school and the elementary schools were completely flooded destroying much of their contents including books and equipment. A new school would have to be built several years later due to the damage from the flood and I was able to be a part of that (more on that later).

The community quickly came together as soon as the flood water allowed and started cleaning

Sheriff Gary McConnell (left to right), Cecil Burk from Rep. Buddy Darden's office, and Harold Peek, chairman of the Trion City School Board, look over the damage to the school by the 1990 flood waters.

Photo courtesy of The Summerville News

up. It wasn't just the people of Trion working to get the schools back in operation, residents from all the county pitched in and helped with the cleanup. It took a week before the school was open and students returned for class.

As the cleanup from the flood continued, we were still faced with our daily job of protecting the county and fighting crime. To aid in the fight against drugs in the county, I joined three other sheriffs in Northwest Georgia and the district attorney of the Lookout Mountain Judicial Circuit to establish a multi-county drug task force in March of 1990. We applied to the Criminal Justice Coordinating Council for a $350,000 grant to fund the project. We were awarded the grant and the GBI provided a supervisor to oversee the program which was based in LaFayette. The task force was comprised of eight investigators representing the counties involved - Chattooga, Walker, Dade and Catoosa.

The task force targeted large drug suppliers and traffickers, as well as assisted each county with drug operations. It was a pilot program for the state. In addition, the task force also worked with the Drug Enforcement Administration (DEA) to arrest and convict major dealers. The program was needed because of the increase in drug activity throughout Northwest Georgia.

Several months later I was surprised and honored when I was named the 1990 Sheriff of the Year. It was presented by the Governor's Criminal

Justice Coordinating Council. This was the second time I had been surprised with this award.

July (17th) of 1990 found the county back in the spotlight with local and area media coverage of another murder.

A pilot program to determine how many crimes were related to drugs was started Jan. 1 (1991) in the Lookout Mountain Judicial Circuit. It was funded by a $50,000 grant from the Georgia Criminal Justice Coordinating Council and a $25,000 grant from the Georgia Department of Human Resources. Sheriff Gary McConnell (left) is shown with District Attorney Ralph Van Pelt (right), who supervised the program, along with Deputy Caroline Cobb, who coordinated the program. The grants were obtained by Sheriff McConnell.

The Summerville News staff photo

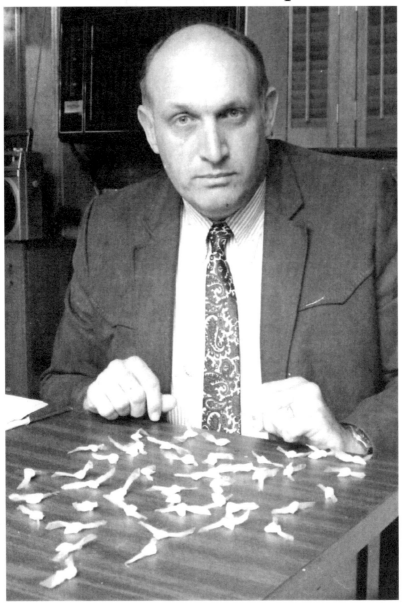

Sheriff Gary McConnell is shown with crack cocaine that was seized during a drug operation. With the times changing, local officers began to find more and more cocaine than the usual marijuana they had once found during drug raids throughout the county. The drug was quickly moving into the county.

Gary W. McConnell

It was election day in July when tragedy struck at one of our poll precincts. I was on my way to the Menlo City Hall, which was the polling place, carrying some breakfast items for the poll workers. It was something I did for all the voting precinct workers throughout the county. I received a call that there had been a double murder - at Menlo City Hall.

Cloudland resident Timothy Brown, 28, had shot his estranged wife, Terri Michelle Brown, 27, and her friend, Gary Sentell, 39, of Gaylesville (AL). Mrs. Brown was the Menlo City Clerk and was assisting with the election prior to the shooting. She was shot in front of city hall and Sentell was shot next door at a gas station.

Brown left the scene and went to the Cloudland residence he had shared with his wife. After ramming his truck into the rear of the residence, he set the house on fire. When we got to the house, we first thought Brown had set the fire and then took his own life inside the residence.

As we investigated, we determined that Brown hadn't killed himself, but had run into the nearby woods. A thorough search by officers on foot, aided by bloodhounds, and by a GSP helicopter was conducted. We put out an all-points bulletin for Brown on a national network. I was contacted by Brown's family the next day and arrangements were made for Brown to turn himself in.

Mrs. Brown had been checking registration

cards when her estranged husband drove up outside city hall that morning. She went outside to his truck where he gave her some child support money. The couple had two small children.

At some point in the conversation, which some say was an argument, Brown got out of his truck. When Mrs. Brown turned and started walking back toward city hall, Brown took a .12-gauge pump shotgun from inside his truck. He turned and fired once toward the gas station where Sentell was. No one knew at the time that he had struck Sentell in the chest killing him.

He began shooting at his estranged wife hitting her several times as she tried to enter city hall. One shot shattered the front glass door of city hall. He followed her to the building, then left her, and returned to his truck. He left the parking lot at a high rate of speed.

The Browns were in the process of getting a divorce when the shooting happened. Brown had been living with his parents and Mrs. Brown had been living in the family home with the couple's 9-year-old daughter and 4-year-old son.

Brown turned himself in and was charged with the murders of his wife and Sentell and arson for the burning of his former home. He was found guilty of voluntary manslaughter by a local jury and sentenced to 10 years in prison. He was released in June of 2001 after serving his sentence.

In early October of 1990 we had a 14-year-old

girl, Christy Lea Stephens, go missing in the Gore/ Subligna area. Her body was found many days later in a densely wooded area about a half-mile from her home.

The young girl had stayed home from school on Oct. 1 complaining of a sore throat. A family member said the last time they saw her, she had turned over in her bed to go back to sleep. Her mother had also been home ill that day. When another family member went to check on Christy later in the day, they discovered her bed was empty and she was nowhere to be found.

A subsequent search for her turned up nothing. Her body was discovered 21 days later by a Marietta deer hunter scouting some property. Her badly decomposed body had been covered with limbs in order to try and hide it.

We secured the crime scene that evening and night until an expert crime scene technician with the GBI State Crime Lab could arrive the next morning. I wanted the crime scene sifted through for possible evidence. The technician did an inch-by-inch search of the area around the youngster's body. He, along with several deputies, crawled on their hands and knees sifting through leaves and soil looking for evidence. We discovered several pieces of jewelry not far from the body.

We had a soaking rain the Monday she was discovered and it was extremely muddy in the area where she was. The deep mud and steep slopes

made it difficult to get to the area without walking or using a four-wheel-drive vehicle. We had to use the winch on the front of the sheriff's department Blazer to help get the stretcher up the slope when we removed her body. Without the long cables of the winch for support, we would have had more difficulty removing her body from the area.

We had a number of suspects in the case, but there was never enough evidence to bring charges against anyone. I'm sorry to say this is one of only a few cases that remain unsolved from my time as sheriff. I had my suspicions as to who the killer was, but unfortunately could never charge anyone.

A few times over the years I've dealt with prisoners in ways I shouldn't have but at the time that conduct seemed appropriate. Back when U.S. Highway 27 was being widened, we had an incident where a man from the Mountain View Community was causing trouble.

The man had commandeered a road grader that was sitting in front of where Stansell's Furniture used to be just before where Highway 27 splits in Trion. The man had a bow and arrow and was shooting at people driving by. I got him off the road grader and put him in the back of my brand new patrol car.

We went several miles down the road on our way to the jail and he kicked the back window out of that new patrol car. We stopped and I had a serious 'discussion' with him, he got back in the

car and we went on to the jail. A few years later he reappeared in my life and reminded me what I had done. More details on this later.

The opening of the state prison finally became a reality in November of 1990. A special dedication program and public open house were held to celebrate the event.

Shirley Miller, who had just become the first lady-elect of Georgia, was the keynote speaker. She was filling in for her husband, the newly elected Governor Zell Miller. She explained that the prison would pump around $42 million into the county economy during a four to five-year period. When fully staffed, it was noted that the prison would employee some 400 people with the majority being residents from Chattooga County with a payroll of almost $10 million per year.

She also praised the late Rep. Forest C. Hays Jr., for whom the prison was named. Hays represented Walker County in the Georgia House of Representatives from 1970 until his death in September of 1987.

During the ceremony I was surprised when I was given a facsimile of a "Time" magazine cover painted by Summerville artist John Turner. Sam Freeman, president of the Chattooga County Chamber of Commerce, gave me the framed "cover." It was presented for my contribution to the county and for my efforts in obtaining the prison.

It's All About The People

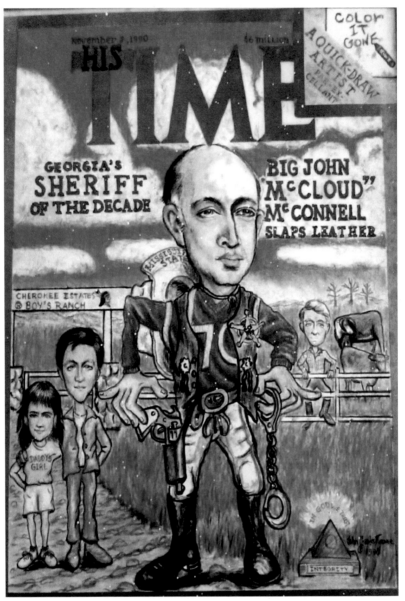

To Gary McConnell
in Appreciation for
Your Community Service to
CHATTOOGA COUNTY

CHAMBER of COMMERCE

Gary W. McConnell

As (Zell) Miller started running for governor and I got more and more involved in his campaign, the Elrod sisters' case bore more on my mind and Becky was getting old enough to be in high school. All this caused me to wonder if being sheriff was the right job for me.

I didn't want Becky to go to high school where her Dad was the sheriff because it may have made her a target for someone to try to get her on drugs or possibly other bad stuff to happen to her through no fault of her own. It didn't, but in my mind the job made her a target for that. I was looking for something different, but not actively, and was struggling with some financial problems from operating the feed store business. Zell and I never once talked about a job. We were good friends and we had helped each other with things as sheriff and lieutenant governor. As the campaign went on, I traveled with him in some parts of the state because my involvement in the sheriff's association and the County Officers Association made me fairly recognizable across the state.

The first time we talked seriously about a job was after the election. The night he won we were at the Peachtree Plaza waiting on the votes to come in. I was up on the stage with him and as he was making his speech for winning. I stepped off like everyone else did. As he started out, now surrounded by security, he walked over and reached over the crowd, shook hands with me and thanked me and said we'll talk in a few days. That few days turned

into two weeks and then we talked.

There were a lot of speculations after Zell got elected as to what I was going to do. There was talk in Chattooga of a special election to fill the office of sheriff and I had to get them (election officials) to slow down because I hadn't resigned yet and wasn't even sure I was going to. I handed in my formal written resignation to Probate Judge Jon Payne on Wednesday, Jan. 9 (1991), and went to work for the Governor on Jan. 14, which was the same day he was inaugurated. When I resigned as sheriff, Probate Judge Jon Payne appointed Chief Investigator Ron Turner to be the interim sheriff until a special election could be held. Payne wanted to appoint someone sheriff who wasn't interested in running for the office and Turner knew he was coming to Atlanta with me.

Looking back on my time in law enforcement, the bottom line is a person must have a commitment to make this job a career. It's not easy. There's a lot of pressure and not just the pressure of hard work or danger. It's the pressure to make sure you're committed to doing the right thing because there are all sorts of temptations out there – from drugs to money to whatever. If you're looking at it just as a job, you're in the wrong business. There are other jobs that pay better for the risks you have to take. But, it's very rewarding because you actually do some good for some people. That's at all levels, not just local but state and federal.

When I left office, I had two unsolved murder

cases in my law enforcement career (over 22 years). In both cases we had a fairly good idea who had committed the murders, but were unable to find enough evidence to make any arrests. There are several reasons for such a good record. First, I had some really good deputies who worked very hard. Second, which I think was a big part of it, I had very good community support. I had a good network of finding out from people what was going on in the county.

There are several people who worked for me during my administration that continue to work at the sheriff's department showing their comittment to serving the public. They are Jerry Davenport, Ken Anderson, Charlie Logan, Tammie Owings, Sam Hancock and Ralph Southerland. There are several former employees who continue serving the public even now.

When joining Gov. Zell Miller's administration I thought that I wanted to be head of GBI. There was some talk about me being the head of State Patrol. He asked me what I wanted to do; I'm sure he already knew what he wanted me to do. We talked a little bit and he said, "I'm going to give you GEMA." Honestly, I had never heard of it. I said, "Can I ask you a couple of questions about that Governor?" He said, "Sure." I said, "What is it, what does it pay, who do I answer to, and do I have a car?" He told me vaguely what it was and what he wanted it to be. He said, "It doesn't matter what it is, this is what I want it to be." At

that time, it was under the National Guard. He called somebody to find out the pay and he said, "Yes, you'll have a car." He also said, "It may take six months or so, but I'll get it out from under the Guard and you report to me." That's where we started and together we built it into a premier emergency management agency in the country.

Soon after taking the Office of Governor, Miller changed a code section of the law to bring GEMA out from under the control of the National Guard. His logic behind the move was because he wanted GEMA to be more active and do more things than it had done in the past. We totally expanded the role of GEMA once it was under the Governor's control. That move allowed you to be more local government driven, more responsive, and to look at a broader range of issues. The Guard is very good at what they do. But GEMA wasn't their core mission. We continued to work with the Guard as they were another state agency that was a part of the state operations plan.

Who would have thought starting out my education in a two-room schoolhouse in a rural Georgia community I would one day oversee an international event with more than 32 million spectators in attendance, 197 countries involved with 11,000-plus athletes participating, and have 30,000 personnel working under my command?

19
My Time as Director of Georgia Emergency Management Agency

Gary McConnell (left) being sworn in as the new Director of the Georgia Emergency Management Agency (GEMA) with newly-elected Georgia Governor Zell Miller (right) looking on.

It's All About The People

Gary W. McConnell

Director

The Governor allowed me to bring three people with me that I wanted as I transitioned into being Director of GEMA. One was Mike Sherberger, who had worked for the Department of Community Affairs in Atlanta. I had worked with him while I was sheriff through the Georgia Sheriff's Association. He was a good writer and good thinker and knew state government very well. Another one was Donna Burns. She had worked for the Georgia

Sheriff's Association for some time and had left there and gone to the Department of Community Affairs. Donna was a good organizer and good 'get it done' person. Ron Turner was the third person I carried after he finished serving as interim sheriff for Chattooga following my resignation. I assigned him to be head of the field operations.

I went down and got sworn in and was taken on a tour of the GEMA facility. I had never been there before. It was in the basement of the National Guard headquarters with no windows. It was sort of like a dungeon. They were as uncertain of me as I was of them. They had one disaster in 17 years. While I was sheriff, we had the flood in Trion in February of 1990, but I never did meet them or hear of them being involved in any way when we were dealing with that disaster. When I went to the GEMA headquarters to be shown around, we went into this room that was their operation center and there were a bunch of tables and chairs. They said, "We've got all these phones and stuff in these cabinets and if something happens we get them out for the people coming in to work the disaster."

Their communication center was like stepping back in time to the 50s when I first went to GEMA. The communication system at the sheriff's department when I resigned was much more advanced than GEMA was when I got there. When I got home that night, Diane asked me, "What do you think?" I said, "When's the next election? If it stays like it is, I'll be running again."

It's All About The People

The Governor wanted GEMA developed into a modern agency and respected nationally. When I left we had taken it to the top making it one of the five premier emergency management agencies in the nation – Georgia, Florida, California, New York and Iowa.

One of the first things I did was try to brighten the place up a little. I got Bill Blackwell and Billy Ray Pursley to come down and paint it just trying to lighten it up a little bit. Then we started reorganizing. I was trying to ease my way into what I was doing. We started making a few personnel changes, moving some people to other areas where they had to be more involved. Most everybody there, especially the supervisors, were on their second careers having retired from the military. They were all nice people, but didn't seem to be very aggressive as far as reorganizing the agency. Their theory was wait until somebody called you before you do anything. They didn't go to a county that had a disaster or problem until the leaders from that county called asking for help.

One of the strange things I found when I got there was that the secretaries and administrative personnel had computers, but the computers were all in one room. The personnel had to get permission from the director to go in there and use the computers. One of the groups I wanted to be able to work well with was the administrative staff, because they knew what was going on, and they weren't all on their second careers. They were

interested in signing on with the new guy and trying to make the agency different. We started putting the computers in where they worked so that they could use them more efficiently.

There were folks working out in the state called field coordinators. At the time there were four and a half for the entire state. How they (the agency) kept up with them was that the field coordinators would give them a three-month calendar telling where and when they were going for that time period. Then if the agency needed to catch up with them, they'd call wherever they were supposed to be at the time and hope they could reach them. They didn't have any communications. I asked the field coordinators what were some things they would like to see changed and communications was one thing they all wanted changed. We were in a meeting in Atlanta and before they left there, they all had pagers. That was at the beginning of portable cellphones. There wasn't a cellphone in the agency when I got there. I got the first bag phone and then shortly after that we got bag phones for all the field people. Legally, GEMA was supposed to be the communications hub for the State of Georgia during any major event.

Three things I remember happening not long after I became Director of GEMA.

1.

We were supposed to have all this power, backup generators and such, to run when all hell

breaks loose. The power went out and I asked, "Why don't we turn the generators on, why are the generators not running?" Their response was something like "Well, we haven't bought any fuel in the last couple of years. We don't have any diesel fuel." The sheriff in me came out and we got some diesel fuel pretty quick.

2.

There was a small tornado in Douglas County February – March '91. The Governor and I wanted to go and see the damage. I told the director of operations, Jim Stockman, "Get me a helicopter. The Governor and I want to go survey the damage." He said, "Well, we can't do that." I said,

GEMA Director Gary McConnell (left to right) talks with Governor Zell Miller and Representative Mickey Channell after surveying tornado damage in Greene County (GA) in November 1992.

"Why can't we?" He said, "Well they haven't called and asked us to come yet." I said, "Get me a helicopter. I'm telling you I want to go and the Governor wants to go. If you can't get it somebody else can." He got me a helicopter. We flew down and surveyed the area. There was damage, not of a massive proportion, but you've got to be there. They (community leaders) can't always call (for help) and most of the time they don't know how to call. That was the first real signal to the GEMA staff that things were going to be different under my administration. I grew up being sheriff, if something happened you went. You didn't wait to

Surveying tornado damage in Greene County (GA) in November 1992 are Quinton Still, Oconee Co. EMA Director (left to right); Gene Autry, GEMA FC; GEMA Director Gary McConnell; Adj. General Bland, Georgia National Guard; Gov. Zell Miller; and Harold Wilson, Greene Co. EMA Director.

It's All About The People

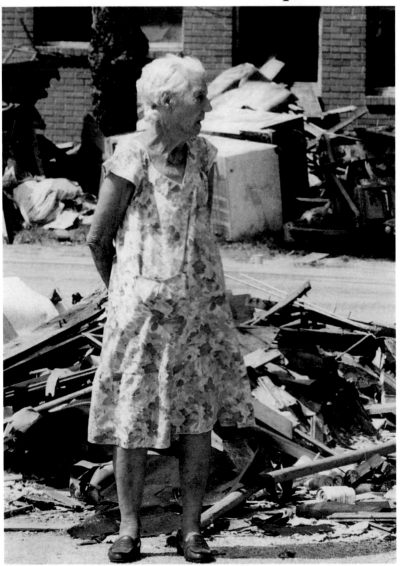

The lady above, a flood victim, stood for who we were working for - the people of Georgia, not a spot on the 6 o'clock news. This photo of the lady was on the wall of GEMA headquarters to remind us of that. I could hardly do a talk on disasters without mentioning her and showing her photo. She reminded me of where our priorities should be and she helped put a face on the disaster instead of just numbers.

be invited.

3.

The next big thing was the flood in South Georgia and the staff was beginning to kind of understand we were going to be a little bit more pro-active. We were starting to make a few personnel changes. We were beginning to change the outlook of things a little bit. We started trying to work more with local governments. If you don't have the support of local governments, you can't survive. You don't have a lot of toys of your own. You control a lot of state toys but as far as having toys with GEMA stickers on them, there were very few, but you have a lot of other stuff. You have to have that relationship with other agencies and departments, Emergency Management is a relationship business.

The first Presidential Disaster Declaration I was involved in as director was in March 15 (1991). Widespread storms and flooding from severe storms struck South Georgia. The flooding was small on the scale of disasters we encountered over the years to come but it was a disaster just the same and it involved 15 counties. It was my first experience working with the Federal Emergency Management Agency (FEMA) and they were very helpful. Not only did they do their job, but they realized I was a new kid on the block and they went out of their way to help me understand the process.

I had been on the board of the Department of

It's All About The People

Public Safety that oversaw the training center which was, and still is, a great place. GEMA did a lot of training for local governments and first responders, but they did all their training at a Holiday Inn off I-20 East. This is where I made another big change. When I told the training director we were going to go to the training center, he said, "You can't do that." I asked him why we couldn't. He said, "We've always done training at the Holiday Inn." I said, "Well, starting the first of the month that's over and we're going to the training center." And they are still training at the Public Safety Training Center.

I remember the first hurricane conference we sponsored. It was in July and we held it in Savannah. We had all the county folks down there from across the state. The head guy of planning had written me a 10-page speech. I had read it and I got up in front of that crowd. I could tell I was just falling flat on my face. They knew a whole lot more about what I was trying to talk about than I did. I finally just pitched the speech on the floor from the podium, walked around in front of the podium and said, "Ok folks. Let me tell you what I want this crowd to be when we grow up. Y'all know all this stuff they wrote about. They wrote a great speech, it's just not me." I just talked to them about what we were going to be, how we were going to get there and I wanted them to be a part of it.

What you've got to remember any time – all

disasters are local. Even the big disasters they're having now, when it's all said and done, the locals are the ones who are going to make it work. The Feds are going to provide a check, state's going to provide a smaller check and a lot of advice. But the nitty gritty hard work, making it work, taking care of the folks, starts at the local level, always has, always will.

What I would tell the local officials I met with was that Atlanta was there to serve them, they weren't there to serve Atlanta. It's true. We were going to get in our vehicles and leave, they were going to be staying there to deal with it and answer for it.

As I became more familiar with the various programs GEMA offered, I called Diane at home to have her look up the term "Mitigation." I also learned about mitigation money using federal funds. A Mitigation Project using federal dollars had never been done in the state. I went and talked with Bill Kinzy, Superintendent of the Trion City Schools. I told him, "I don't know if we can do this or not but if you are interested I think we can get you the money to build a new school." The Trion schools had been damaged badly by the 1990 flood.

We had to have matching funds to make the project work. After meeting with the school board Kinzy and I, along with Harold Peek (Chairman of the school board), called Robert Pamplin, owner of Mount Vernon Mills and told him what

the situation was. Mr. Pamplin told us he'd give the matching funds and the school was built. We presented the Trion Board of Education with a letter of credit from Gov. Miller for $800,000 to be used in building the new school. The Governor came up and opened the school. This was the first time, but not the last, that Mitigation Money was used for a project.

To further help the Trion City School System, the Georgia National Guard did the grading work for the new school. Inmates from the Hays Correctional Facility helped the system landscape the new school site.

GEMA Director Gary McConnell, Georgia Gov. Zell Miller and Trion School Superintendent Bill Kinzy stand in front of the newly dedicated Trion City School. The school was rebuilt through funds provided by the state and matching funds following the disastrous flood of 1990.

Gary W. McConnell

Also during this same time the Tillotson Corporation (which owns and operates Best Manufacturing, a glove manufacturing firm in Menlo, GA) agreed to donate a 14-acre site to the town of Menlo, provided that a sports complex be built on the site. While they were working on the Trion school, the Guard's grading team also did work at the Tillotson Sports Complex on Highway 48 in Menlo. The grading allowed construction of a new ballfield, a parking lot, and a basketball court. They also helped with a drainage ditch, installation of a lighting system, and installed a septic tank and field line system.

Inmates from the Hays Correctional Institution Boot Camp helped with the landscaping,

A formal presentation of an $800,000 grant to Trion City Schools from GEMA was made. On hand for the presentation were (seated, left to right) Roy Brown, Lester Griffitt, Johnny Ingle, Dale McCollum, and J.W. Greenwood; (back row) Larry Stansell, June Grose, Roy Bowers, GEMA Director McConnell, School Board Chairman Harold Peek, Trion Mayor Allen Plunkett, and Trion School Superintendent Bill Kinzy.

built a block maintenance building, a press box and concession stand, as well as helping with the bleachers. They also built a pavilion at the ballfield. I was honored that the Menlo Recreation Department named one of the baseball fields after me.

Official groundbreaking held for Menlo Facility. On hand for the event were (left to right) Rep. Buddy Darden; Pam Hegwood, co-director of the Menlo Recreation Department; GEMA Director McConnell; George Mack, Best Manufacturing; and John Crawford, Hays Correctional Institution Boot Camp.

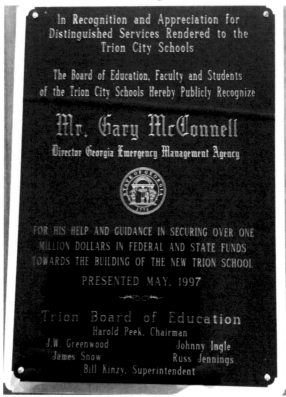

This joint project was the first of its type in the state and was part of Gov. Miller's commitment to put state resources to better use. The National Guard assisted as part of their Domestic Action Project which was designed to assist local, state and federal agencies alleviate social and economic problems in the community.

Over a course of time, county officials throughout the state began calling for assistance with various things. They learned we were there to help them. We put in a 1-800 number for them to call when needed without them having to pay for it. In a few years as technology advanced, we developed a website and gave everyone access to it. It was very similar to the way I ran the sheriff's department. If we heard of something happening in South Georgia (or any part of Georgia), I was on my way. It may have not been in a copter or fixed

wing plane, I may have been driving. We didn't wait for them to call us for help. They seemed to appreciate that, even if there wasn't much we could do for them. We were there to support them at least.

Emergency management, not just in Georgia, but across the country may not actually elect a governor, but you can certainly defeat one by not doing your job. Governor Miller understood that and so did Governor Roy Barnes after Miller. Later, Miller was President of the National Governors Association and they always met with all the new governors elected to let them know what to expect. Miller told the group the most important appointment you're going to make is the emergency management director. He said you may not think so right now but they will have more to do with your future than anyone you appoint. That's the person more people have contact with in bad situations.

We continued to modernize the agency with equipment, better training for personnel and trying to build relationships with city and county governments across the state and other state agencies. Working with the County Commissioners Association and the Georgia Municipal Association, we started going to their annual meetings and doing training on emergency management. Some of the training was just general overview and some was very detailed in case something happened they'd know what to do.

Gary W. McConnell

We improved communication systems and moved upstairs in the National Guard building in 1994 after the National Guard moved out.

In 1995 we totally remodeled the state operations center and brought in all new technology and at the same time, the state was preparing to build the new traffic management center (pre-Olympics). Steve Parks, the number two guy at DOT, and I came up with this idea to build the traffic management center adjacent to the operations center and tie all the technology between the two agencies together. They did and that's where they still are today.

A little before that, we had entered into an agreement with the Department of Natural Resources, the Department of Transportation, and the Department of Agriculture to combine all the communications in our communication center. So, we basically turned into the 911 center for the state of Georgia with the exception of law enforcement. That was a little before we built the transportation center. Honestly, combining communications center was driven by necessity because we were running out of money to run the radio room. By combining those it gave us the resources to build a first-class communications center. We managed it; it was in our building. Some of the personnel worked for the various agencies, but they all reported to us. At the same time, we brought in communications for the civil air patrol.

This was a one step at a time thing, it wasn't

overnight. We were making a little progress every day. "It's got to be better when you leave it than it was when you found it or you are wasting your time."

One of the main things GEMA does basically for emergency management is to maintain the state-operation plan for major events, natural disasters, man-made events. What that means is that you work with the other agencies to assign responsibilities during an event so they will be trained for it, equipped for it and prepared to do it.

Each one of the state agencies, and some of the volunteer agencies in the private sector, all have an assigned person to work at GEMA to do their respective part. Not all of them come there every day, but that's their job. For example, agriculture had a full-time person assigned to emergency management. They were in charge of livestock, agricultural products, and fuel. The Department of Agriculture regulates fuel in Georgia. Which means if you're running out of fuel on the coast in a hurricane, it's Ag's responsibility to figure out how to get it down there. That's just one example.

Keeping those plans updated, exercising them so everybody understands how they work, and finding out what's not working and fixing it is GEMA's very complicated job description. The same thing is true with the nuclear power facilities in and around Georgia. GEMA and DNR (Department of Natural Resources) have the

responsibility for those.

DNR is involved because they have the Environmental Protection Division (EPD). The way that was structured allowed them the monitoring of the nuclear release and then our lead was the coordination of the evacuation, reentry and training of the local government.

There are two nuclear facilities in Georgia – one in Waynesboro (Burke County) and one in Appling County - and the one in Dothan (AL) is right on the state line so it's shared between us, Alabama and Florida. Now, we also have the Savannah River Nuclear Facility.

The next major disaster was the March blizzard of 1993 when I-75 was shut down all the way from Valdosta to Chattanooga (TN). There were power outages in some places for up to six weeks. There was also a tremendous amount of traffic backlog on the interstates.

We had had tornadoes in Polk County. I left GEMA and went by Cedartown to close the application center because the tornadoes had happened about a month earlier. I came on home that night and the blizzard hit during the night. Nobody could go anywhere. I got the National Guard to send a helicopter to Chattooga to pick me up. I had to go from my house to the farm to get a field big enough for them to land. In the process of doing that in my personal vehicle, I busted the windshield out hitting a tree going down the side

of the ridge.

The Guard picked me up. In the chopper was Adj. Gen. Bill Bland of the Georgia National Guard and myself. We flew to Chattanooga to get re-fueled and then flew to Atlanta, where we picked up Gov. Miller and started basically flying the interstate trying to figure out what to do with the roads. The interstates looked like they were filled with Tinker Toys with all the tractor trailers turned every which way, as well as the cars.

We landed in Calhoun at the National Guard Armory and there were some college kids stuck on the side of the road when we got off the chopper.

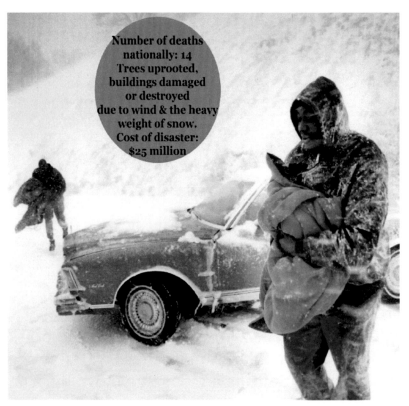

Number of deaths nationally: 14
Trees uprooted, buildings damaged or destroyed due to wind & the heavy weight of snow.
Cost of disaster: $25 million

Gary W. McConnell

We had a pool photographer with us. Gov. Miller went over and started pushing on the car and that made national headlines, the Governor on the side of the road pushing a car in the snow.

Trying to get the power back on and get the interstates back open were the two main priorities, along with supporting the hospitals and nursing homes. There were a lot of trees down, basically all across the state.

I remember one funny thing. We got two National Guard companies to help with the utilities because they had long reach equipment that they could get into places the utilities companies couldn't. I was telling the governor, "We've got two National Guard companies out helping in rural North Georgia to get the power back on." He said, "Well Gary, I know one of them is in Chattooga. Where's the other one?" I said, "Well Governor to be honest, the other one is in Young Harris (the governor's home town)." He said, "I always thought you knew what you were doing." Those were two of the rural areas hardest hit and were justified to have the help.

During my entire career (sheriff, GEMA, and after), I fully believe that these things have happened in progressive order. Little one, little bit bigger and it just continuously grew. If you look at it, we had the small flood in '91, had a couple more in '92, blizzard of '93 (that was a challenge), then the floods of '94 which was (and is) <u>the worst natural disaster the State of Georgia has ever had</u>.

233

It's All About The People

That was sort of the climax of disaster building. We had a lot of other big events after that, but they weren't that big (unless it was your house that was damaged). We didn't have another one that big where that many counties were involved in the same disaster. There were 55 counties involved in the '94 floods.

In the threat of floods, tornadoes, hurricanes, blizzards, terrorism, nuclear disaster, and other massive emergencies, GEMA took the lead in coordinating state, national, and private non-profit resources to prevent and alleviate suffering.

A railroad bridge in Bibb County (GA) over the Ocmulgee River where flood waters floated a train off the tracks.

Gary W. McConnell

A flood victim holds his Bible as he surveys what the flood waters have done to his home and the surrounding community.

235

It's All About The People

From 1990 to early 2003, GEMA responded in Georgia to 12 presidentially-declared disasters/emergencies, including four tornadoes, five floods, one hurricane, and one snow-storm. In excess of $500 million in federal aid was directed to alleviate the suffering of the victims in these disasters. GEMA oversaw more than 150 State of Emergencies.

Tropical Storm Alberto drifted inland in July of 1994 and relentlessly dumped rain from Atlanta to

Baker County Courthouse in Newton was flooded by the Flint River. The courthouse, built in 1906, was placed on the National Register of Historic Places in 1980. The courthouse had previously been flooded in 1925 and 1929.

the Florida Panhandle and the Alabama gulf coast. Miller called it "the single most severe disaster in the history of the state."

Alberto took 34 lives, left 50,000 homeless, had water the color of coffee to rise 25 feet over flood stage that burst dams and wiped out farms, roads, railways, and businesses. The cost of the disaster was $425 million.

GEMA led the massive coordination of relief efforts, which took many partners, including 20 state agencies, to respond to the urgent need of victims.

With rivers rising as quickly as one foot per

Aerial view of a typical community in South Georgia flooded by Tropical Storm Alberto in 1994.

hour, some victims escaped with only the clothes on their backs. GEMA secured and assisted in distributing 10 million gallons of water during the 22 days. Macon and Bibb County were out of water due to flooding of the Macon Water Authority.

During the days without water, no vital health services – dialysis, nursing homes or hospitals – were forced to shut down. GEMA brought in tractor-trailers, tanks of water, bottled water, water purifiers, generators and pumps to maintain pressure and to keep these services operating.

Deral Dukes, GEMA field coordinator for 28 counties, with other GEMA staff and the Federal Emergency Management Agency (FEMA) set up Disaster Assistance Centers (DACs), where flood victims could enroll in assistance programs offered through various agencies represented at each DAC. Victims visited DACs, for example, to find lodging through the Red Cross, register for unemployment through the Department of Labor, and sign up to receive food stamps through the Department of Family and Children's Services. DACs were open 12 hours daily.

Coordinating the delivery of drinking water, food, supplies, and finding places for victims to sleep were just a few of the ways GEMA and FEMA helped the flood victims. The agency sent people to aid the government with "city business" like locating a place to keep the shipments of bottled water after the water supply was contaminated. The agency also helped provide some 4,700

trailers for temporary housing for the residents left without homes due to the flooding. That included securing the trailers, but also securing a place to set up the trailers, setting the trailers up with water and electricity; and making it accessible to the residents with roads.

GEMA continued to coordinate the work of helping Alberto flood victims long after the initial response was over in the form of "buy-out" programs. This is where the federal government bought flood-prone land from homeowners who then relocated to higher ground.

We were in Albany after the '94 floods during the heart of the campaign for the governor's re-election in November. Zell had tried to change the flag and couldn't; he was in political trouble. We were standing on the runway at the airport in Albany (GA) waiting to get on a state plane. This was probably two weeks into the flood maybe a little longer. It was just me and him. He said, "Gary, you ever thought about running for Governor?" I said, "No (and hadn't). Why?" We had 55 counties in the disaster area. Everything from the Atlanta Airport south to the Florida line, west of I-75 and a few counties east of 75. He said, "Well, whether you know it or not, you're running right now. How you do in these 55 counties will depend on whether you and I can walk into the Capitol next year or not." I thought, *Well, why don't you put a little pressure on me?* He said, "Just remember that when you're making these decisions." Then

he followed up with, "Can you fix this?" I said, "Yes sir, we can fix it." I said, "I don't know how we'll pay for it." He said, "It ain't your problem to pay for it, it's your problem to fix it. I'll worry about paying for it. If we get beat, somebody else can worry about paying for it."

From that point on he never, ever questioned me about the amount of money I was spending in a disaster. We spent a lot. But that's what it takes to make it work. You can't go to a disaster and say, well I'll have to check and see if I can make this happen. You have to go knowing you have the support to make it happen when you get back to Atlanta. He was very good at not only telling it but, through his actions. Right after we started we had a big dinner meeting at the mansion. He had all the agency heads and their number two and three staff. I sat down and he sat down and said come over here and sit next to me, they need to see you sitting next to me. He called the meeting to order and thanked everyone for coming. As a surprise to me, he said, "I'm turning this meeting over to Gary. He's running this. He's running the disaster. Y'all have any questions or any concerns, see him and if he needs to talk to me about it, he can." What I'm saying is it takes everybody and we did build a good organization and we built a good Emergency Management Agency.

During that flood crisis of 1994 Gov. Miller, Sen. Sam Nunn, me and I think Sen. Paul Coverdell were flying in South Georgia. President Bill Clinton was

out of the country in Poland on some kind of trip. He and the Governor needed to talk, and we were on a plane in Taylor County. We landed there and the sheriff, Nick Giles, picked us up and took us to his house because he lived close to the airport so that the President could call the Governor.

There were two <u>funny</u> things about that. The sheriff's wife was having some kind of bridge club at their house where they were playing for money. The sheriff had to call his wife to tell her to clean off the table, the Governor was coming to the house.

When we got there, Nick's 12-year-old son was home too. The President was going to call the Giles' home from Air Force One on his way to Poland. The sheriff told everybody we were waiting on that phone call and to leave the phone alone. The young boy went to his bedroom unbeknownst to any of us at the time. Nick answered the phone, it was President Clinton and he handed it to the Governor. They talked and hung up. A few minutes before we left, Nick's son came back into the room and his daddy said, "You know who that was on the phone, son?" The young boy said, "Yeah, it was the President. I was listening on the extension in the bedroom." That was an embarrassing time. First, the sheriff had to tell the women at his house to clean the money off the card table because the Governor was coming. Secondly, his son was eavesdropping on the Governor and the President.

Not long after that on the same day, we were on a helicopter - Miller, Nunn, Coverdell, myself,

Adjutant General Bland of the National Guard, and a pool reporter. We got into some really bad weather and had to land. We just found a clear spot where they had been clear cutting pulpwood and landed because there were some really bad storms coming through. Gen. Bland looked at me and said, "You know what would happen if this thing crashes?" I said, "Yeah, we'd all die." He said, "Past that?" I said, "No." He said, "The headlines will read Gov. Miller, Sen. Nunn, and Sen. Coverdell killed in chopper crash along with <u>others</u>. I don't want to be others. You and I won't even get our names mentioned, we'll just be others."

When the water treatment plant was out in Macon, we were having to haul water to the hospital. We were hauling three million gallons a day, that's all we could haul. What the hospital did was have everyone flush like Dr. Pepper - 10, 2 and 4. We just couldn't haul any more water. That was all the trucks we could find.

We had to have 10,000 Porta-Potties and nobody in the state or surrounding states had them. I ended up buying 10,000 Porta-Potties from a company in California, but they said it was going to be two weeks before they could deliver them. No, it wasn't going to be two weeks. We needed them right then. When all was said and done, we bought two tractor-trailers in California and flew some DOT (Department of Transportation) drivers out there to drive the trucks and Porta-Potties back to Georgia so we could get them as soon as possible.

After we finished using the trucks, we turned them over to DOT. The state needed the Porta-Potties, we got them, and hauled them home. Coordinating the delivery of drinking water, food, supplies, and finding places for victims to sleep were just a few of the ways GEMA helped those in need.

The river was almost at the interstate from Exit 169 to downtown Macon. We had 175 miles blocked on the interstate because the bridge over the river was out. Going up a hill to the bridge, there were tractor trailers and cars stranded. It resembled a car lot. One of the tractor trailers was hauling BBQ grills and another was transporting steaks. As we flew over you could see people in the middle of the interstate cooking steaks on these grills for everybody that was stranded out there. That was just one of many ways people came together to help each other during disasters.

Governor Miller and I flew for 17 continuous days during the flood. I don't know how many days I flew total during that tragedy. There were 55 counties touched by the flood. We would fly into a county, meet with the local officials that our advance team had gathered together and find out their top five needs at the time. We knew there was a lot they needed, but we couldn't do everything at once.

During the floods, the County Commissioners Association sent out a notice to the governments in South Georgia regarding what to expect. Here's

It's All About The People
how they explained it:

Local government leadership as never before...

Flood in Georgia

"You will be challenged in the next six months as never before in your lives," Gary McConnell so warns local government officials in more than 40 flood-damaged counties of southwest Georgia.

On Sunday morning, July 10, the weary director of the Georgia Emergency Management Agency propped on his desk at the EOC (Emergency Operations Center) in Atlanta and told hastily assembled representatives of local government organizations his assessment of the flood situation. It was still developing, of course, with the flood crest on the Flint River just passing Albany at a record level and heading for Bainbridge.

McConnell and his lieutenants had been flying the region by helicopter for most of the daylight hours since July 4, dropping down to check on preparedness for the most urgent hazards, the rescues, searches for missing citizens, weakened dams, destroyed bridges, drowned cities and railroads, Interstate Highway 75 had to be closed for the first time ever. He summed it up in a few sentences:

"This is the greatest disaster to occur in Georgia in recorded history. Many, many Georgians have suffered the worst event of their lives, and

it continues...Parts of cities will have to be totally demolished.

"It is apparent from what we have observed the last few days that we are going to have to rebuild the southwestern one-quarter of Georgia. From Columbus south to the Florida line, from I-75 west to Alabama. These hurting communities need leadership out of local government as rarely ever required of them before," he stated.

Georgia Gov. Zell Miller (left) and GEMA Director Gary McConnell discussing the damage done by the flood waters in South Georgia.

It's All About The People

As Georgia responded to the flood emergency, people were the first priority: their rescue, evacuation, shelter and food. The local and state emergency agencies were able to handle that early imperative in short order with shelters and assistance from many community volunteers. By the fifth day of the emergency, however, local EMA personnel, public safety and public works employees were becoming exhausted.

The procedure for emergency management is for the community suffering the disaster to use first its own resources, then to call on GEMA to mobilize the state's resources. The third level of help comes from the Federal Emergency Management Agency (FEMA) which, with prescribed documentation, will reimburse the state and localities for many of their disaster-related expenses.

By the fifth day of flooding brought on by tropical storm Alberto's torrential rains, GEMA personnel had been working 15-hour shifts and some 'round the clock, dining almost exclusively from vending machines in the EOC bunker and from lunch packs which the Department of Corrections prepares in large quantities for inmates working outside state prisons. They were dealing with the greatest workload they had ever encountered, and with damage of unprecedented magnitude in Georgia. "Not even Sherman could have done this," groaned one observer.

ACCG Executive Director Jerry Griffin saw

much of the destruction first hand as he flew with state and federal officials to some of the worst flood areas and talked with county officials on site.

As the crisis spread down the Flint and Ocmulgee river corridors, from an initial four counties to more than 40, GEMA called on ACCG, the Georgia Municipal Association, Georgia Sheriffs Association, congressional staff support and other state agencies to help identify resources to help the stricken area. Jerry Griffin immediately loaned his assistant director, Ross King, to GEMA to match up resources from other governments with those in need. With the loss of public drinking water supply and wastewater treatment in many communities, there was an urgent need for alternative sources of such services. Counties and cities in the flooded area lost the use of some sanitary landfills at the time when flood debris removal would present landfills with unusually high volume. King would be searching for alternative waste sites, among other things.

Meanwhile, offers of help were pouring into GEMA, ACCG, and GMA from counties and cities outside the disaster area. On July 11 McConnell's staff were organizing a county "Outreach" effort to match up donors and needy recipient governments. ACCG has a key role in that. Road-building equipment and supplies, portable pumps, water tanks, portable toilets, building inspectors, engineers, surveyors, public works and public

It's All About The People

safety personnel are high on the needs list (which ACCG will continue to publish for the next several months). Officials of possible donor counties and cities should contact ACCG at 404-522-5022 or Ross King at GEMA (County Assistance Office), 404-624-7048.

Watch for updates of this information by FAX or mail from ACCG. Telephone contact numbers may change.

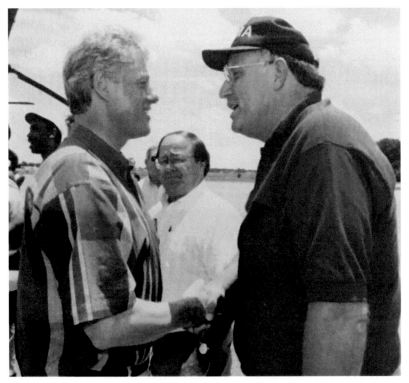

A brief moment away from politics and problems discussing simple things like cowboy boots. Talking with President Bill Clinton (left) on the runway in Albany (GA) about Lucchese cowboy boots which we were both wearing at the time.

Gary W. McConnell

We had to prioritize GEMA, so I asked them to give me their five most important things to get their community back productive. The requests ranged from getting their water treatment working to getting their roads open to pumping the water out of the courthouse. In Baker County, which is south of Albany, the water was in the second floor of the courthouse. In Bibb County (Macon), a lot of their people worked at Warner Robins. The state highway getting them there had five bridges out on it. That was one of their five top priorities even though they knew we couldn't snap our fingers and have their bridges fixed. We did get started on it. We had to know what they needed. What I

Talking with U.S. Senator Sam Nunn during the preparations for Tropical Storm Alberto in July 1994. The storm resulted in 34 deaths, 50,000 homeless, and cost $425 million.

thought might be the most important, might have been 25[th] on their list of needs.

Like in Albany, this was longer term, they had five schools washed out, totaled. We started bidding out and we finally got two or three bids out. Construction got started and then we had to quit for a while simply because we were driving the price up on ourselves. There was such a demand for what we were wanting done, that the contractors were supply and demand. We built three schools and then had to wait until later to build the other two schools. We had to bring in 4,200 manufactured homes for the residents in the Albany area. We had to build water and sewage lines, as well as streets, lease land and build from scratch.

One of the days we were flying, we were in Montezuma and had been flying all day. We landed near a Hardee's and got some hot dogs. We didn't even take time to eat them there, we got back on the chopper and headed out again. It was the governor, me and the pilot. The governor and I were eating our hot dogs and the pilot looked at me and said, "Gary here, fly this thing. I can't eat my hot dog and fly this thing." He told me not to do anything besides "hold it still."

Here I was flying myself, the governor and this pilot while he's sitting there eating a Hardee's hot dog.

Another time we were flying a state fixed wing

Discussing the flood situation with Georgia Senator Max Cleland (left to right), SBA Director (standing), FEMA Director James Lee Witt, and Georgia Gov. Zell Miller.

plane down in Upson County. We were going to land on a grass airstrip and it was in a pasture. The pilot said, "Okay, we're going to have to buzz the airstrip first." We had to run the cows off the airstrip. The first flyby they all went running and we circled back around and landed where we had run the cows off from.

The Governor's wife, Shirley, is just a super nice lady. When we were flying every day for those 17 days during the floods of 1994, I was picking the Governor up every morning at the mansion for our daily trip. One morning when I went to pick

him up, we landed the chopper out in the yard and I went to go get him. Shirley met me at the back door and said, "Gary, you had anything to eat?" I said, "No ma'am." This was later on in the morning. She said, "Come on in and let me make you a sandwich." I thought this lady is the First Lady of Georgia. She didn't go have someone else make me a sandwich, she made it. She said, "I'm going to make you a sandwich. Zell's not quite ready." We sat down in the kitchen and I ate that sandwich that Mrs. Miller made. She is just the sweetest lady you would ever want to meet.

During the floods I had an encounter with a gentleman that I had dealt with during my days as sheriff. You may recall the story I mentioned earlier about the guy on the road grader with the bow and arrow that I had a confrontation with which lead to him being a bit bruised. Well, I ran into him during the floods. You never knew how a conversation was going to go when you meet someone you had dealings with as sheriff and they asked, "Did you used to be sheriff?" I told him that I had been and that I recognized him.

He said, "I just want to tell you something. You got all these problems in South Georgia and I got six tractor-trailers. Whatever you need them for, you let me know. It won't cost you a penny. I'm successful today because you kicked my ass." I kind of grinned and he said, "You kicked it really well." The guy had become very successful in the trucking business. We did use some of his tractor

NATIONAL WEATHER SERVICE

**SOUTHERN REGION
DIRECTOR'S PARTNERSHIP AWARD**

Presented to

**Georgia Emergency Management Agency
Director Gary McConnell and Staff
and
The Governor's Task Force on
Warning and Communication**

For outstanding efforts and dedication to
the expansion of NOAA Weather Radio
coverage in the State of Georgia.

February, 2000

X. William Proenza
Director NWS Southern Region

trailers, but we paid for their use.

I shouldn't have done what I did to him when I was sheriff, but it did have a positive effect on him. It made him think about what he was doing and where he was going. It was wrong for me to do it, but at least it helped him get on a path to a better life. It makes you feel good that you might have actually helped someone.

Each event helped us to get better organized, get more people, to have better training, and to also bring other state agencies together. This is a partnership, it's not just GEMA. For example, in '94 the governor's race was going on at that time. The flood destroyed 177 voting precincts across the 55 counties. We had to go in and build 177 temporary voting precincts. That was done by the National Guard and Department of Corrections. Corrections is a major player. They have plenty of equipment, officers, and inmates who can do manual labor under strict supervision.

There is a role you can find for everybody in a disaster. One of the big roles in South Georgia during the floods was body identification where the caskets came out of the ground. The Georgia Bureau of Investigation (GBI) ran that. Special Agent Lee Sweat oversaw that operation.

Re-interment was another aspect that had to be dealt with to find a place where they came from outside the floodplain that is satisfactory to the local community and their relatives is a very

GEMA's mobile commications vehicles (above) are used throughout the state when disasters strike.

tough job. A law is in place now that would require identification on caskets to help in disasters such as this.

GEMA does more than just respond to tornadoes, ice storms, and floods. Georgia is faced with all forms of natural and man-made disasters, along with the increased risk of terrorism. When the unthinkable becomes reality, GEMA personnel goes into action helping to assist local authorities in responding to whatever the emergency is. Furthermore, GEMA is on the scene until the community is back on its feet helping in any way they can.

Another area GEMA helped residents was when Gov. Miller formed the Task Force on Warning and Communications. The group studied the communications and warning systems needed to protect Georgia residents during severe weather

such as tornadoes.

This lead to more than 20,000 NOAA (National Oceanic and Atmospheric Administration) weather radios being distributed to area schools, hospitals, nursing homes, courthouses, and day care centers. It also led to more tower facilities being installed in various parts of the state (including one atop Taylor's Ridge in Chattooga County) to provide better coverage for the NOAA Weather System to reach all residents of the state.

We also created the Severe Storms Research Center and acquired a mobile communications vehicle to enhance emergency response capabilities. These critical projects were a part of GEMA's comprehensive and proactive program of preparedness and mitigation.

On Oct. 22, 1997, 11-year-old Levi Frady went missing on his way to his home in Forsyth County (GA) after a day of playing with friends less than a mile from where he lived. The youngster's body was found the next day in the woods of a neighboring county. He had been brutally murdered. (His murder has never been solved.)

In his memory, GEMA and the GBI created Levi's Call, a program to get the word out to the public when a child goes missing. The goal of the program is to locate the child and the abductor quickly before any harm comes to the child.

Levi's Call is an investigative tool activated only by local law enforcement agencies through a

Levi's CALL

request to the GBI when an abduction is confirmed. The GBI then contacts GEMA, who is in charge of getting the word out to the public regionally and statewide. The alert is broadcast by radio and TV stations, along with being placed on digital road signs.

Gov. Miller also initiated the Governor's Public Safety Awards (GPSA) in 1998 to recognize the outstanding accomplishments and efforts of the men and women of Georgia's public safety community. The program highlights acts of heroism or oustanding deeds which resulted in saving lives and protecting property; and for outstanding job performance which enhances their profession. The annual event identifies two individuals from each discipline of public safety, as well as two state government employees. The program is to honor those men and women while they are alive, as the state already had a program to honor those who gave their lives in service to the state and the people of Georgia.

The people behind these stories are the backbone

It's All About The People

of our state's public safety. They are the heroes of today and the legends of tomorrow. That first year more than 80 public safety personnel from all over Georgia were nominated for the awards. Twenty-one state and local public safety personnel from around the state were honored at the ceremony.

The first awards ceremony was held at the Georgia Public Safety Training Center in October of 1998. The GPSA Monument dedication ceremony coincided with the awards presentations. The

The Governor's Public Safety Award Medallion

monument is engraved with the recipients' names.

Gov. Miller told the crowd at the awards ceremony, "This program is our gift of thanks to all the public safety personnel who have made a commitment in their life to serving the citizens of the State of Georgia. Often we take for granted our safety, and every once in a while we need to be reminded of the individuals who make our safety a priority."

The need to address the problem of school violence was becoming clear in 1998. GEMA

Gov. Zell Miller (right) and GEMA Director Gary McConnell are shown with the Governor's Public Safety Awards (GPSA) Monument which was unveiled during the first awards ceremony in October of 1998 at the Georgia Public Safety Training Center. The monument is engraved with the GPSA recipients' names.

took on the responsibility of developing a comprehensive program not only to prepare for the possibility of school violence and to ensure a prompt and effective response, but also to take every step possible to prevent it.

GEMA's efforts were bolstered even further in 1999 when Gov. Roy E. Barnes passed into a law a

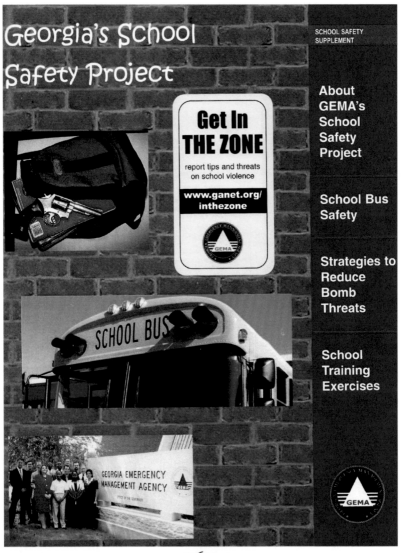

measure requiring every public school in Georgia to develop and implement a comprehensive school safety plan that addresses the entire gamut of risks including the potential for natural disasters, weapons, gang activitiy, drugs, bomb threats, and

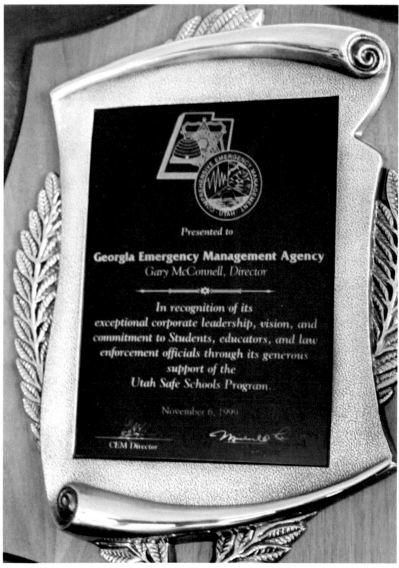

A plaque of appreciation where I assisted in helping Utah set up their own Safe School Program.

acts of violence.

GEMA is charged with providing a model safety plan as a guide for local schools, providing training and technical assistance to schools that are preparing their plans, conducting site surveys and responding to school incidents.

GEMA's school safety coordinators trained education, emergency management and public safety personnel on a broad array of subjects including crisis management planning, bomb threat management, search and seizure protocols, and visual weapons screening.

The development of our school safety program led GEMA to aid other states in setting up their own programs dealing with school safety and violence.

Another program through GEMA is the Excess Property Program which enables state and local law enforcement agencies to acquire property no longer needed at miliary bases. The U.S. Department of Defense initiated an Excess Property Program in 1990 to support the President's National Drug Control Strategy. The intent and purpose of the program was to acquire excess property from the various branches of the military and give it to local law enforcement agencies to be used for the purpose of combating and preventing drug distribution.

Georgia began participating in the program in 1991 and GEMA was appointed by Gov. Miller as the executive agent for the program.

Gary W. McConnell

Examples of equipment provided to various law enforcement agencies throughout Georgia as part of the Excess Property Program.

It's All About The People

GEMA Director Gary McConnell (right) makes presentation to Summerville Mayor Sewell Cash of a mobile command unit as Summerville Police Chief Tony Gilleland looks on.

From boots to bulldozers, socks to airplanes, excess property is requested and tracked through a computerized system documenting need and availability. Law enforcement agencies are eligible to apply for equipment, which is allotted based on criteria requiring that it be used in counter-drug and counter-terrorism activities. GEMA disbursed millions of dollars worth of equipment through the program to agencies throughout the state.

In just one four-year period, we were able to provide the Chattooga County Sheriff's Department some $178,836 worth of equipment. We also provided over $91,000 to the Lookout Mountain

Walker County Sheriff Al Millard (left to right), Catoosa County Sheriff Phil Summers, and Chattooga County Sheriff Ralph Kellett, members of the Lookout Mountain Judicial Task Force, look on as GEMA Director Gary McConnell briefly explains the Excess Property Program and introduces Gov. Zell Miller. Gov. Miller presented military four-wheel drive trucks to District Attorney Ralph Van Pelt, chairman of the Lookout Mountain Judicial Task Force; Glynn County Police Chief Carl Alexander; and Newton County Commission Chairman Davis Morgan (representing Sheriff Gerald Malcolm) during a ceremony on the west plaza of the State Capitol.

Judicial Circuit Drug Task Force in equipment during that time and more than $37,300 worth to the Trion Police Department. We were able to provide well over $111,500 worth of resources to the Summerville Police Department.

This equipment included such items as various vehicles, a four-wheel drive Army surplus truck, and a 100 kilowatt capability generator just to name a few.

Chattooga wasn't the only county to benefit from the Excess Property Program, but it was nice to be

These helicopters were provided to the Atlanta Police Department through the Excess Property Program.

able to provide needed items to the local agencies.

As an example of agencies benefiting from the program, Gov. Miller presented "free" four-wheel drive trucks to Glynn County Police Chief Carl Alexander, Newton County Sheriff Gerald Malcolm, and District Attorney Ralph Van Pelt, chairman of the Lookout Mountain Judicial Task Force. These agencies received the 199th, 200th, and 201st four-wheel drive trucks to be distributed through GEMA to law enforcement agencies for use in the continuing effort to fight drugs in the state.

While severe weather has long been a major focus of GEMA, we drastically expanded GEMA's role as the state led emergency preparedness agency to face the potential threats of domestic terrorism and weapons of mass destruction. I served as the chairman of the Governor's 911 Committee where we were responsible for setting

Gary W. McConnell

Chattooga County Sheriff Ralph Kellett (left) with a new generator presented by GEMA Director Gary McConnell (right) through the Excess Property Program.

training and equipment standards for 911 services in local communities. Similarly, GEMA developed training standards for private search and rescue dog teams across the state.

We began another program in 1998-99 called the 911 Program recognizing youngsters throughout the state who did something outstanding by calling 911.

GEMA had just become the lead agency for the 911 Center in the state. We got with Lt. Gov. Mark Taylor and we asked all the 911 Directors all over the state to submit names of youngsters who had really done something outstanding by calling in or reporting an emergency.

We had a board, which I chaired, to select the

267

winners. We selected winners from all over the state of Georgia. We would bring the winners to the Capitol during the Legislation and they would be recognized in the House on the floor, get their picture made with the Lt. Governor, get a medallion, and various other items like caps, tee shirts, etc.

Coke furnished the caps and Georgia Pacific and McDonalds furnished the tee shirts, while lunch was provided by Chick-fil-A. The youngsters were recognized for their contribution to public safety.

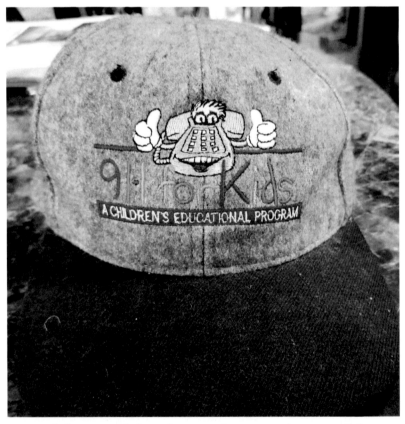

One of the caps (above) was given to winners of the 911 for Kids Program during their visit to the Capitol to be honored.

Gary W. McConnell

The Albany (below), GA and surrounding areas had over 300 caskets to come out of the ground (like above) causing many to open up. This required recovery of bodies, identification, and burial. There were 50,000 people left homeless and the cost of the disaster was listed at $425 million.

Photos by The Albany Herald

It's All About The People

There are times you have to just take a break. This was a rare moment with Governor Zell Miller at Christmas. We both enjoyed wearing Lucchese cowboy boots so I gave him a pair with his name on them as a Christmas gift. He's showing those off as we take a break in his office.

GEMA staff (left to right) Bill Blackwell, Field Delivery Personnel; Janice Tittle, Administrative Assistant; Lisa Ray, Public Affairs Director; GEMA Director Gary McConnell; and Vonya Bartlett, Senior Administrative Assistant.

Gary W. McConnell

A reminder that those caskets lost in the flood are not forgotten.

President Bill Clinton talking with workers during the floods in south Georgia. Standing in foreground is Janie Griffin, GEMA representative.

20
Crime Lab Groundbreaking

The creation of a Georgia Bureau of Investigation (GBI) crime laboratory in Chattooga County began in 1995 and became a reality June 4, 1996, with the ground breaking ceremony near the Hays Prison.

I was extremely honored that the facility was named after my dad. The lab was named the John Frank McConnell Regional Crime Laboratory.

There was a tremendous back log of cases at the crime lab in Atlanta, and had been a problem during my sheriff's career. When I was on the Board of Public Safety under Gov. Joe Frank Harris, I began talking to Robbie Hamrick, director of the

The official groundbreaking ceremony at the John Frank McConnell Regional Crime Laboratory.

Gary W. McConnell

Gary McConnell (left to right), Diane McConnell, Becky McConnell, GBI Director Melton "Buddy" Nix, and Johnny Crawford.

Gary McConnell (left to right), former Chief Deputy Sheriff Bert Tucker, Rep. Tim Perry (from Chattooga County), and Chattooga County Commissioner Jim Parker.

It's All About The People

At the crime lab groundbreaking with Vernon Keenan, who is a long time friend and at the time was Deputy Director of the GBI. Vernon is now the Director of the GBI.

GEORGIA BUREAU OF INVESTIGATION

JOHN FRANK McCONNELL
BRANCH CRIME LABORATORY

DEDICATED TO THE MEMORY OF
JOHN FRANK McCONNELL
(1913 – 1967)
WHO SERVED THE CITIZENS OF CHATTOOGA COUNTY
THROUGH HARD WORK WITH HONOR AND INTEGRITY

ZELL MILLER
GOVERNOR

MILTON E. NIX, JR.
DIRECTOR, GBI

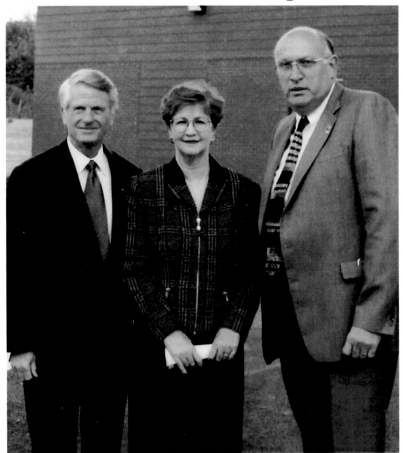

Gov. Zell Miller (left) with Diane and I at the crime lab dedication service honoring my dad.

GBI at the time. Robbie and I got to be (and still are) close friends. I talked to him about the need for another crime lab and he agreed.

The Department of Corrections had bought the property in Pennville for the state prison and still had some available property after the facility was built. I talked with Bobby Whitworth, Director of Corrections, and asked if they would be willing to transfer ownership of that extra property to the

GBI. He was agreeable to transfer the property to the GBI for them to build a crime lab.

It took several years for the crime lab to become a reality as the process came in phases. Gov. Miller finally kicked it over the line for us. This was also during the time when Tom Murphy was the Speaker of the House. Murphy and Rep. Johnny Crawford (from Lyerly) were good friends and that helped. Murphy also had a connection to Chattooga County because his brother was the last Railroad Agent in the county at Lyerly.

Most people don't understand, it's a network of activity to get things accomplished in government.

Through Rep. Tim Perry's work, the Legislation passed a resolution naming the crime lab after my dad. Gov. Miller was the keynote speaker at the dedication service and Milton E. Nix Jr., director of the GBI, was the master of ceremonies.

Also speaking during the dedication ceremony was Summerville attorney Bobby Lee Cook. Cook told the crowd, "The McConnell name has become synonymous with law enforcement. John Frank McConnell brought integrity, dignity, and stability to the sheriff's office that was needed at the time."

"John Frank was endowed with the values of family, duty, and home and he possessed a great sense of individual fairness," Cook continued. "I can think of no more fitting tribute than for this building to be named in his honor."

It's All About The People

In speaking to the lab employees, Cook concluded, "If you can serve as he did, then this laboratory will serve as a taproot for a free and democractic republic."

When I spoke to the crowd, I told them the reason I was there that day was "because I'm Sheriff McConnell's boy." I also shared with the crowd the story my dad told me when I was a 16-year-old feeling my oats.

Dad told me to draw a bucket of water from the well, get a glassful and stick my finger in it. He told me when I took my finger out, if the hole was still there then "you're an important person." That was the way my dad was.

GBI Director Nix told the crowd that the new crime lab was a critical addition to the state system to keep up with the increasing demands of the state.

The facility served 13 Northwest Georgia counties and cost $3.4 million. The lab allowed law enforcement agencies in the 13 counties closer access to drug, fingerprint, and firearms identification; DNA analysis; blood alcohol determination; toxicology services; and trace evidence comparison.

The crime lab operated until March of 2010 when it was one of three labs selected to be closed due to declining state revenue, according to then Georgia Gov. Sonny Perdue. The other two facilities were in Columbus and Moultrie.

Gary W. McConnell

Gov. Perdue's supplemental budget that year recommended shutting down the three facilities to save state funds. The facility in Chattooga County remains empty and the property ownership has been transferred back to the Department of Corrections.

More scenes from the crime lab dedication service on the following pages

It's All About The People

Peter Boney Sr. (left to right), Gary McConnell, and Mr. and Mrs. J. P. Smith.

Georgia Gov. Zell Miller (left) speaks with Summerville attorney Bobby Lee Cook following the crime lab dedication ceremony.

Gary W. McConnell

Summerville attorney Bobby Lee Cook (standing) speaking at the crime lab dedication service.

Georgia Gov. Zell Miller (above) speaking at the dedication ceremony of the John Frank McConnell Regional Crime Laboratory in Chattooga County.

It's All About The People

A large crowd was on hand for the dedication ceremony of the John Frank McConnell Regional Crime Laboratory in Chattooga County.

The McConnell family (Gary, Becky and Diane) following the dedication of the John Frank McConnell Regional Crime Laboratory in Chattooga County. Dr. Marlin Payne in the background.

21
THE 1996 OLYMPICS

The State Olympic Law Enforcement Command (SOLEC) merged the efforts of 29 State of Georgia public safety agencies with GEMA leading the one-team approach to providing security for the massive 1996 Olympics in Atlanta.

The Olympics was the largest peacetime event

in history at that time. The Atlanta Games would be larger than the combined games of Seoul, South Korea, and Barcelona, Spain.

GEMA's remodeled State Operations Center (SOC) served as the hub of all public safety activities. Available were 100 work stations with computer and voice capability, computerized weather prediction, and live video feeds from venues, aircraft and the state Department of Transportation's system of cameras.

It was very important to have a place where all the agencies could gather and work together.

SOLEC, GEMA's arm of public safety coordination, extended to Gainesville, Savannah, Athens, and Columbus. GEMA staffers manned three mobile command posts for the games throughout the state.

In Gainesville, GEMA staff members were sent to help at the rowing venue. All the inlets and entrances to the area were monitored by the Georgia Department of Natural Resources and the Georgia State Patrol to ensure that no unauthorized person entered.

In an innovative project to keep the public safe by managing the heavily traveled air space above the Games, GEMA joined in a partnership with the Federal Aviation Administration (FAA) and the aviation industry, led by the Helicopter International Association. Placing Global Positioning Systems (GPS) on board helicopters,

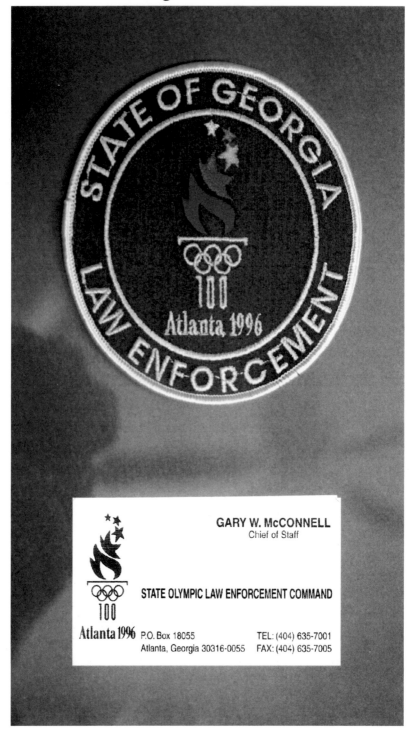

the demonstration project allowed air traffic to be monitored and air space to be better managed.

Known as the Regional Disaster Emergency Management System (RDEMS), the test project has implications for future use in response to emergencies, particularly those requiring precise and immediate coordination of aviation and ground assets. The system could significantly decrease the response time to emergencies requiring choppers to transport victims for medical care.

Although the Olympics offered the chance for GEMA to showcase its services, the agency's daily leadership in coordinating the preparation for and response to emergencies is equally impressive.

At any given time, we had some 5,000 public safety personnel working for SOLEC each day. They were living in an apartment complex downtown or in Lakewood Manufactured Homes. We delivered mail, operated a hospital, and built a fire department among other things for the personnel preparing and overseeing the Olympics.

We set up a post office so that the workers' mail and packages could come to one place, and we could deliver it out to them. We leased and set up manufactured homes, built our own fire department, and built our own restaurant out there. We even had a bus route to deliver the workers to their jobs. We didn't use the public bus system in Atlanta, we had our own bus system. We also had a route to deliver food to everyone on their job

site. We had to manage where people lived since you didn't want people working different shifts sharing an apartment or disrupting an apartment complex.

In addition, we borrowed two school buses from the Trion City School System that the FBI used for the Games. The buses were pre-wired in case we had a hostage situation where the criminals demanded a way to escape. With the wired buses, we could monitor the criminals if need be without them knowing. The buses were de-wired and returned to the Trion School System after the Olympics.

Members of SOLEC (left to right) Buddy Nix, Director of the Georgia Bureau of Investigation; Col. Sid Miles of the Georgia State Patrol; Adj. General William Bland of the Georgia National Guard; and Gary McConnell, Director of State Olympic Law Enforcement Command.

It's All About The People

During the Olympics, SOLEC transportation system traveled more than 65,000 miles in buses and vans delivering 1,700 officers to work and used 15,000 gallons of gasoline. The U.S. Department of Defense supplied $14 million in equipment consisting of 20,000 hand-held radios for Olympic security, 1,500 pagers, fax machines and telephones. In addition, 180,000 Child ID Tags were distributed to help prevent the number of lost children. There were some 500,000 cups of water, along with hats, fans, and sunblock given out at eight heat prevention centers inside the Olympic Ring to park visitors.

The Olympics were for 17 days and the Paralympics were 10 days after that, plus the Paralympic torch run. All the planning for the Games took four years.

For me, overseeing GEMA stopped in January 1996 when I became the director of SOLEC. The Governor appointed (Mike) Sherberger acting director of GEMA and I was no longer responsible for the day-to-day operations; I only had SOLEC to worry about.

SOLEC was a stand-alone agency out of the Governor's Office. I had my own support staff. I took quite a few people with me from GEMA. We relocated our operations.

Col. Sid Miles of the Georgia State Patrol; Buddy Nix, director of the Georgia Bureau of Investigation; and Adj. Gen. William Bland of

the Georgia National Guard, were still in charge of their departments' activities. The day-to-day operations of SOLEC and all the decision making was basically mine. I was the chief of staff to the Governor.

I inherited overseeing the Olympics from Stock Coleman, who went on to direct the Torch Run throughout the United States. He did a great job with the Run going through 48 states, over 15,000 miles. He and his crew of about 40 people made the event a huge success. Local resident and former Representative Johnny Crawford was a member of the security detail that traveled across the country with the Olympic flame. The detail was a complicated event with timing, location, and coordination with all the jurisdictions you had to go through.

Every aspect of the Olympics was our responsibility from start to finish. This meant from the time it touched down in California, until the time another torch was lit and handed back to the Olympic Committee to be returned to Greece for the next Olympic Games.

The Governor and I, along with several others, flew out to Los Angeles to receive the Olympic torch at the LA International Airport. We took it by helicopter into the Los Angeles stadium where the torch run began. It ended in Atlanta at the stadium with Muhammad Ali lighting the flame for the Games to begin. All the planning, all the routing, all the security – everything from the time

It's All About The People
♋♋ The 1996 Olympic Torch Relay ♋♋
Presented By
Coca-Cola

The map above shows the route the torch relay took across the United States before arriving in Atlanta for the Games. The map below shows the torch route throughout Georgia before arriving at the Games.

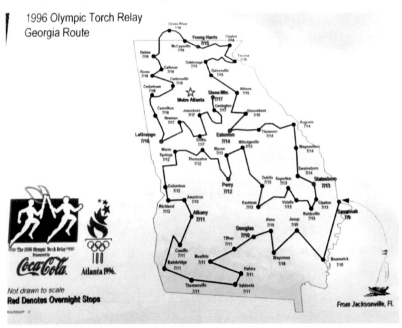

1996 Olympic Torch Relay
Georgia Route

Not drawn to scale
Red Denotes Overnight Stops

that plane landed at the airport until the torch got to Atlanta, was ours.

There were a couple of funny things that I remember about the torch run. When we got to the airport, this very pretty lady representing a Greek Goddess brought the torch off the plane and presented it to us. Right before we left, while we were still on the tarmac, I looked and there was the so-called "Greek Goddess," sitting on the tailgate of a pickup truck in her goddess tunic smoking a cigarette. I don't know why, but that just struck me as funny.

We had several back up torches that were supposedly lit from the Olympic flame in Greece to use to relight the torches in case the flame the runners carried went out. Somewhere in Oklahoma a big Indian Chief was taking the torch across a lake in a canoe. The canoe turned over, dumped the Indian Chief in the lake and put the torch out. As I said, we had a backup flame just in case something happened. You just don't think about an Indian Chief tipping a canoe over out in a lake.

I call Vicksburg (MS) kind of my second home because of Mother, so Diane and I went to Vicksburg to see the torch run. The torch came into town on a train, was taken off and made its way through town before returning to the train. The train continued on to the Mississippi River where it stopped on the bridge and a big fireworks display was held. It was pretty amazing!

It's All About The People

The next time we saw the torch was in Huntsville (AL) where Diane, Becky and I ran in the Torch Run. After that I didn't see the Olympic Flame until it came into Savannah on a Tall Ship. I was with Governor Miller and other officials on hand to welcome the Torch Run to Georgia in a special ceremony. From Savannah it made its way through the state before arriving at the Games in Atlanta.

The night of the Olympic's Opening Ceremony dress rehearsal I had some tickets and Diane, along with several couples from Chattooga County, came

After my time running the Olympic Torch, I lit Diane's torch for her run. She in turn lit Becky's torch. We ran the torch relay in Alabama.

down to watch. I walked up as they were getting ready to watch and I got a call on the phone while I was there. Security personnel thought there was an explosive device on the other side of the stadium from where we were. It was like five minutes before

Becky McConnell running in the 1996 Olympic Torch relay.

the event started. I said, "See y'all, I have to go."
I walked down and was going to walk across the
field. A security guard said, "Sir, I don't know who
you are but you can't go. This is about to start." I
said, "Unless I get over yonder, this isn't going to
start" and I told him who I was. We walked across
Opening Ceremony grounds about three minutes
before it started. We got over there and found out
there wasn't anything to it.

During the 17 days of the Games, if you averaged
it out we responded to a reported suspicious
package every 10 minutes around the clock for
the entire 17 days. Not all of them were live, but
you didn't know it until you got them disarmed.
And unfortunately, one of them went off. We had
venues all over the state, so it wasn't just metro
Atlanta.

The night of the explosion at the Atlanta games
was the fourth night, 1:20 a.m. on Friday morning.
I was sleeping at the operating center; I had living
quarters there. They came in and woke me and told
me what happened. So, I got to make three or four
calls – the Governor, both United States Senators,
and the President. When I called the President, I
told him who I was (I'm sure whoever answered
the phone had already told him too) and I had met
him a couple times before. I said, "Mr. President, I
just talked to the Governor and he wanted me call
you and tell you what has happened at the Games."
So, I told him. He said, "Okay, tell the Governor
I'll call him." I called the Governor back and I said,

The Olympic torch was officially brought into Savannah on the ship above.

Georgia Gov. Zell Miller (center) lighting the Olympic torch in Savannah before the flame made its way to Atlanta to officially begin the games.

It's All About The People

"I just talked to President Clinton and this is what he said." I said, "Expect a phone call from him."

You have to remember these Games were held before all the extreme tight security we have today where bags have to be clear to be allowed in a venue. In fact, the Olympic Organizing Committee didn't want any extra security in the Centennial Park since it was a venue open to the public with or without tickets. Until after the explosion, there weren't any check points in Centennial Park.

After the explosion, we brought in 750 more deputies from around the state and three sheriffs to oversee them. We gave them training so that they could be efficient in the field. We also set up check points around the Park. You didn't have to have a ticket, but you did have to go through a check point after the explosion. We set the

A scene from the Olympic Games.

metal detectors tighter. We had sufficient public safety personnel at all of the other venues. We just became even more vigilant in the overall safety procedures.

The public became more aware of hazards too. Deputies were searching bags as people were going into the park. There was a youngster about 10 years old who had a backpack on and the deputies didn't search his pack. The youngster asked the deputies, "Why would you not search mine (meaning the backpack)? Please search mine too."

The search for the bomber was a joint effort between federal authorities, state and local authorities. It was a joint effort between several federal law enforcement agencies led by the FBI

An aerial view of Centennial Park during the Olympic Games.

with support from state and local authorities. The search turned into a large manpower drain, especially when it was learned the bomber was hiding out in the mountains of North Carolina. It took a long time to locate him there.

The bomber, Eric Robert Rudolph, spent five years on the run before he was caught in 2003. He was arrested by a city policeman in Murphy, N.C., behind a grocery store at night. Rudolph was apparently dumpster diving for food as he had been hiding in the nearby mountains. As part of a plea bargain, Rudolph plead guilty to numerous charges and accepted consecutive life sentences.

PARALYMPIC GAMES

We had the Paralympic Games to oversee just 10 days after the Olympics ended. There weren't as many venues and they weren't as widespread across the state as the Olympics. There weren't as many countries involved and not as many athletes participating. Security remained in place even though the attendance wasn't as high, and the attention wasn't as visible. The security was just as tight, but the threats weren't as high.

The Paralympics ran from Aug. 16 through Aug. 25. The games in Atlanta was the first time the Paralympics received mass media sponsorship and it was also the first time the Games were televised on American TV.

There were some 100 nations represented at the Games with some 3,260 athletes participating.

Gary W. McConnell

The torch run for the Paralympics traveled an average of 100 miles a day and went through four states. An estimated 1,000 hands relayed the torch on its way to Atlanta. The torch was lit from the Martin Luther King Jr. Eternal Flame in Atlanta before winding its way back to the stadium.

The athletes were just as focused as the athletes in the Olympic Games and they were just as intent on winning as the other athletes had been. I had to admire them more because of the issues they were having to deal with besides trying to win.

Georgia Gov. Zell Miller (right) with Blaze, the mascot for the Paralympic Games, and SOLEC Director Gary McConnell.

It's All About The People

All of the athletes for the Paralympic Games were amazing. There was one athlete I remember very well. He was a swimmer who I watched during a practice session before the Games. He was a triple amputee and was also blind. There was another athlete who was running up and down the side of the pool with a fishing pole that had a tennis ball on the line hanging in the pool. The pole was for when the blind athlete came to the end of the pool because he couldn't see when to flip and go the other way. The other athlete kept the tennis ball out in front of the swimmer so when he reached the end of the pool he would touch the tennis ball with his head and know to flip for his return lap.

Looking back over the Olympic Games Gov. Miller said, "*Success for the state was more than just gold medals. It was being able to provide a safe and enjoyable environment for the citizens*

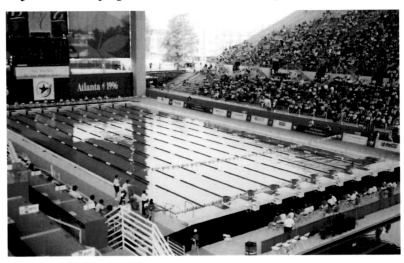

A scene from the Paralympic Games.

Photo Courtesy of Lee Sweat, SOLEC

of Georgia and all its visitors. Because of your individual dedication and desire to help achieve our goals, the 1996 Olympic Games were a very proud moment in our state's history. I applaud your efforts as part of one of the finest law enforcement teams ever assembled for one event."

Col. Sid Miles, Commissioner of the Georgia Department of Public Safety said, "The 1996 Olympic Games united local, state, and federal law enforcement together with the National Guard and Military to form an unprecedented security force. America can be proud of how these professionals formed the foundation for the success of the 1996 Olympic Games."

Milton E. Nix, Jr., Director of the Georgia Bureau

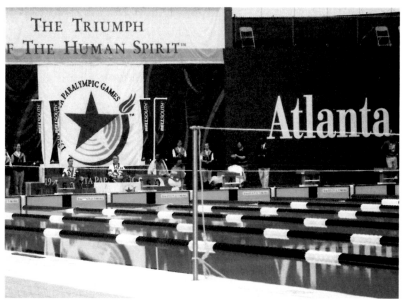

The athletes in the swim competition of the Paralympic Games were amazing to watch.

Photo Courtesy of Lee Sweat, SOLEC

of Investigation, added, *"The 1996 Centennial Olympic Games were an enormous success from a public safety perspective as a result of the cohesive and professional partnership of so many agencies. The success of Olympic public safety operations is attributed to the effective and efficient coordination of the participating agencies, and to the dedication of each individual who made it their personal mission to secure the 1996 Olympic Games."*

Major General William P. Bland, Jr., Adjutant General of the Georgia Department of Defense, concluded, *"SOLEC was state government at its finest - outstanding cooperation between all state agencies."*

My thoughts on the games were, "The 1996 Centennial Olympic Games required a total public safety effort, combining all state personnel and resources under one unified command, SOLEC. This command, encompassing 29 state agencies required the total commitment and cooperation of agency heads, as well as the hands on involvement of the Governor."

Because of my experiences with the Olympics, Centennial Park, the abortion clinic explosion and The Other Side Lounge where all three had a secondary device used, I was recognized at one time as knowing more about terrorism than anybody in the United States. Along with the U.S. Department of Justice, we did a training video about secondary devices. We did that right after

the Games in '96 and they distributed nationally to every public safety agency and it is still being used today.

That was the first-time secondary devices had ever been used in this country against law enforcement. They were used at the abortion clinic and The Other Side Lounge. At the abortion clinic, if a couple of GBI agents hadn't just parked where they did, there probably would have been five or six officers killed. The second explosion was next to a trash can in the parking lot where they were standing and the cars were just in the way. Then the Other Side Lounge, an alternative lifestyle lounge in Atlanta, was the third target. We actually found that secondary device on a dirt bank and disarmed it.

If you look now at all this terrorism, the thing they are really worried about is secondary devices. Take the Las Vegas Strip Massacre on Oct. 1, 2017; even as bad as it was, when they found the shooter's car it was booby trapped. It was a secondary device designed to kill officers or anyone nearby.

It goes back to starting in Atlanta, Georgia, in 1996. The same thing happened at the World Trade Center. When the first plane hit, the firemen, the law enforcement, and the EMTs rushed in and then the second plane hit. The second hit is where most of the First Responders lost their lives.

In 2006, after I had gone to work with IEM, we were doing a National Plan Review in Wayne

It's All About The People

County (Detroit), MI. I was doing a presentation for the Wayne County Law Enforcement. During a break, I heard training going on in the adjacent room and it was me talking.

I walked over to the next room and they were actually doing training on secondary devices using the video we (at GEMA) had done about 10 years earlier. I don't know who was the most surprised - I was there and walked in a class while they were watching a video I was speaking in, or the class where the guy in the video walked in the room while they were watching the video.

I returned and finished the class I was doing and then went back to the second classroom that afternoon. I talked with them for awhile and gave them some additional information that wasn't in

Speaking before the United States Senate encouraging them to create Homeland Security, as seen on C-Span 2.

the video.

In my capacity as GEMA Director I spoke before the United State Senate at a hearing before Homeland Security was created. My role there was to represent the Emergency Management Directors across the country. Senator Joe Lieberman from Connecticut was chairman of the Senate Committee that was overseeing the hearing. Georgia Senator Max Cleland introduced me to the panel.

My testimony was about how diluted the federal government was to get assistance to state and local governments. There were so many different agencies doing so many different things that you spent a lot of your time saying, okay is it the Department of Agriculture, Health and Human Resources, FEMA, or the Veterans Administration that handles this particular issue.

Our push at the time, and it later happened, was to create what is now called the State Authorized Representative, in which most cases it was the Emergency Management Director. It was here in Georgia and I was the State Authorized Representative.

That's when they created Homeland Security on a national level to funnel all the information through one point. That doesn't mean Homeland Security was handling the grants for Ag, for example. They were the conduit to get you where you needed to be. You had a single point of contact

and didn't need to know someone in Ag to obtain assistance. My job was to try to get them to do it (Homeland Security) then and not talk it to death.

Some two years after the Olympics I had the pleasure of doing something that was an honor to me, but might surprise others how important it was to me and how much I really enjoyed doing it.

I've spoken in a lot of places. Over the years I've spoken in Italy, Salt Lake City, Chicago, Washington, D.C., New York, Los Angeles, and Boston just to name a few places to audiences of all sizes filled with all types of business and

I was the keynote speaker at the 1998 graduation exercises for the Chattooga High School (above). Some 138 seniors received their diplomas.

government leaders and dignitaries. But the one event where I was the guest speaker that has a special meaning to me, is when I got invited to be the commencement exercise speaker at the Chattooga High School by the 1998 graduating class. Student Chris Jarrett invited me to speak and introduced me.

That was one of the neatest things I ever got to do, especially here locally, to come back and be the speaker at the high school graduation commencement. It was the only time I have ever spoken at the local high school graduation.

There was a Chattooga High School Hall of Fame and in 2010 I also was inducted into that. I received a really nice plaque and they also placed a plaque in the Hall of Fame section at the Chattooga High School.

That year it was me; Sewell Cash, who served as

In 2010, I was also among the inductees into the Chattooga High School Hall of Fame along with (left to right) Sewell Cash and Joe Kines.

mayor of Summerville; and Joe Kines, who went on to coach in the SEC. There was a good turnout for the event, which was also a fundraiser for the high school football team. A reception was held prior to the banquet for the families of the Hall of Fame inductees and the 1969-71 football players and cheerleaders. It was a nice surprise.

While I had a busy schedule as GEMA Director, I also made every effort to keep learning. In 1999 I became a member of a Harvard class that met two weeks every quarter through 2003.

The class, Executive Session on Domestic Preparedness, was made up of a variety of leaders from all over the United States.

I was the guest speaker at a dedication service honoring public safety personnel hosted by Sheriff Jackie Barrett of Fulton County, Georgia.

Gary W. McConnell

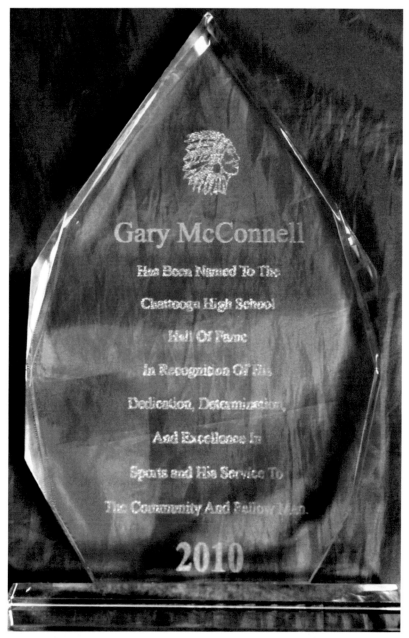

The Hall of Fame award presented to me by the Chattooga High School in recognition of my "Dedication, Determination, and Excellence in Sports and Service to the Community and Fellow Man."

It's All About The People

HARVARD UNIVERSITY

JOHN F. KENNEDY
SCHOOL OF GOVERNMENT

Executive Session on Domestic Preparedness

December 1999 - February 2003

In recognition of and with special thanks to

GARY MCCONNELL

Arnold M. Howitt
Director

Juliette N. Kayyem
Executive Director

 Executive Session on Domestic Preparedness
December 1999 - February 2003

Gary W. McConnell
Olympic-related moments

Vice President Al Gore talks with Chief of Staff Gary McConnell of SOLEC at a pre-Olympic meeting in Atlanta, GA. Looking on are Sheriff Jackie Barrett of Fulton County and Woody Johnson, Special Agent in Charge of the FBI Atlanta Office.

ATLANTA
1996

Centennial Olympic Games

Presented in appreciation to

Gary McConnell

for outstanding cooperation in support of
the protective responsibilities of the
United States Secret Service
during the 1996 Summer Olympic Games
in Atlanta, Georgia

Eljay B. Bowron

Director, United States Secret Service

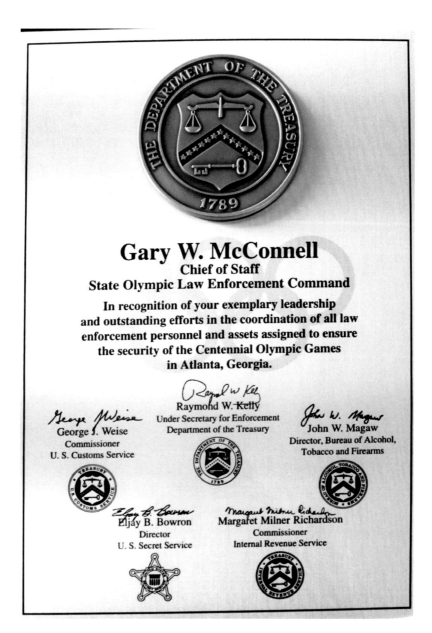

Gary W. McConnell
Chief of Staff
State Olympic Law Enforcement Command

In recognition of your exemplary leadership
and outstanding efforts in the coordination of all law
enforcement personnel and assets assigned to ensure
the security of the Centennial Olympic Games
in Atlanta, Georgia.

Raymond W. Kelly
Under Secretary for Enforcement
Department of the Treasury

George J. Weise
Commissioner
U. S. Customs Service

John W. Magaw
Director, Bureau of Alcohol,
Tobacco and Firearms

Eljay B. Bowron
Director
U. S. Secret Service

Margaret Milner Richardson
Commissioner
Internal Revenue Service

22
A NEW ADMINISTRATION

After serving his maximum two terms (eight years) as Georgia Governor, Zell Miller left office when Roy E. Barnes was elected the new governor in 1998.

Gov. Miller went on to serve the people of Georgia as US Senator from 2000 to 2005 before retiring from public service. Sadly, he passed away in 2018.

The McConnells and the Millers. Serving with Gov. Miller for eight years was a pleasure despite all the hard work. Our families sharing some time at the Governor's Mansion (left to right) myself, Shirley Miller, Diane, Becky, and Gov. Miller.

Gary W. McConnell

Gov. Barnes took office in January of 1999 and asked me to remain with his administration in my capacity as director of the Georgia Emergency Management Agency. I agreed and continued working for him and the people of the state as I had done for Gov. Miller.

One of the most formidable challenges we faced in the early part of the Barnes' administration, was the Y2K phenomenon. The concern was that more and more we were becoming dependent on computers for so much of our operations.

David Saye (left to right), director of the Georgia Public Safety Training Center; Georgia Governor Roy Barnes; and Gary McConnell, director of the Georgia Emergency Management Agency.

It's All About The People

Since no one could accurately predict the consequences of the Y2K problem, we had to be prepared. We didn't believe it would be catastrophic, but we knew there would be some problems or interruptions in vital services and that we had to be ready to handle them.

Gov. Barnes appointed Mike Hale director of the Y2K Program Management for the state. At the same time, we at GEMA had to develop a contingency plan for the coordination of resources to respond to possible emergencies that might arise. We had already started a series of workshops around the state to collaborate with local elected officials, public safety and public works managers, representatives of the utilities and others to

Vice President Al Gore with tornado victims, along with Gov. Barnes, Congressman Sanford Bishop, and GEMA Director McConnell.

identify potential problems, and made plans on how to respond to them.

We also had to be prepared to deal with public perception of the Y2K issue. The fear of the unknown can be a powerful force and people were already beginning to stockpile items.

The expertise, professionalism and commitment of everyone involved in addressing the issues of Y2K paid off. The consequences weren't as bad as had been predicted by some.

We also saw our share of natural disasters during

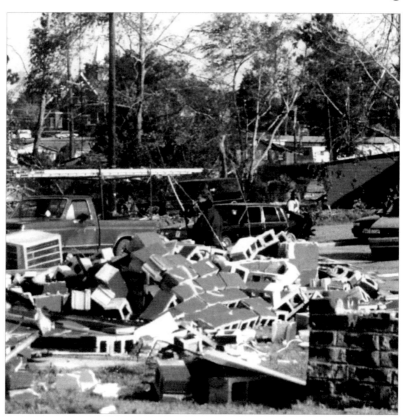

A scene from the Dooley County tornado.

It's All About The People

Gov. Barnes' administration, such as tornadoes, hurricanes, flooding, and numerous other types of disasters.

On April 20, 1999, a Presidential Disaster Declaration was issued for Chandler and Dooley counties after a tornado ripped through them. There were at least 24 people injured as a result of the tornado. Numerous businesses and approximately 65 homes were damaged or destroyed by the twister. The cost of the disaster was an estimated $3.8 million.

There were other disasters we handled such as a State of Emergency in Carroll County in August of 2000 due to severe drought conditions. State financial assistance was used to help rent pumps

Gov. Barnes, myself, Vice President Al Gore, and Senator Max Cleland, along with state and FEMA staff, surveying storm damage in South Georgia.

and develop a well.

The following September, GEMA assisted the City of Monticello with purchasing raw water from a private reservoir. Faced with water shortages, GEMA also facilitated the installation of an emergency water line and pump to assure that Hays State Prison had access to water.

Drought conditions continued with limited rainfall creating a prime environment for wildfires in May of 2001. Thousands of acres of forest land were destroyed in six Southwest Georgia counties. GEMA coordinated state response efforts and worked to secure a Federal Fire Suppression

GEMA Mobile Command Operator Woody Davis (left to right) and GEMA Field Coordinators Vickie Thompson and Sandy Land with former President Jimmy Carter in Plains, GA.

It's All About The People

Grant to reimburse costs for the McIntosh County wildfire that destroyed more than 4,500 acres.

GEMA also worked with coastal counties in obtaining Economic Disaster Injury loans from the Small Business Administration when Georgia shrimpers suffered severe economic losses as a result of adverse weather conditions.

GEMA's mobile communications vehicles (MCV) are deployed at a moment's notice to areas where communications capabilities have been disrupted, bringing necessary services such as cell phone, landline phone, and satellite radio capabilities.

2002 Wayne Shackelford
Award
Presented to
Gary W. McConnell

23
TRI-STATE CREMATORY

Georgia was back in the national and international spotlight in 2002 when state authorities discovered that the Tri-State Crematory

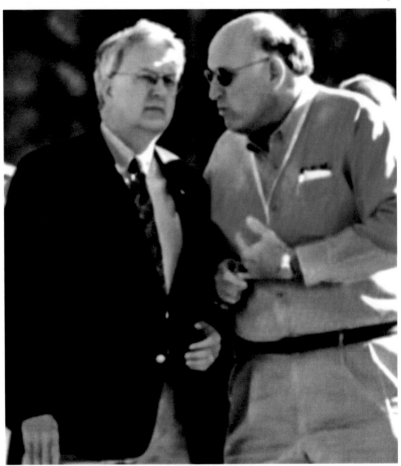

Discussing the situation with Gov. Roy E. Barnes (left) on the crematory property in the Noble Community.

This was the scene we found at the Tri-State Crematory. Caskets were just sitting out on the ground.

in the Noble Community north of LaFayette in Walker County, GA had not been cremating bodies appropriately. More than three hundred bodies were found dumped throughout the crematorium property rather than properly cremated.

The EPA in Atlanta received an anonymous tip that something unusual seemed to be going on at the crematory operated by Ray Brent Marsh Jr. Authorities investigated and found piles of rotting human bodies in vaults, scattered throughout the property, and in a storage shed.

GEMA sent in disaster teams and began trying to identify the remains. This was difficult because most of the bodies were in advanced stages of

decomposition with many being little more than skeletons. It appeared that over the years the families of the deceased had been given concrete dust, dirt, and other material instead of cremated remains. Marsh claimed the cremation oven had broken, but a reason for his actions concerning the bodies was never given. Families from some 37 states were touched by this tragedy.

Within hours of the discovery, both of GEMA's mobile command vehicles were on site. I notified Gov. Roy Barnes of the situation. He declared a State of Emergency on Feb. 16 (2002) to allow state resources to be used on private property. GEMA coordinated the response. The agencies involved in the effort were DPS, GBI, GSP, DOT, DNT, Consumer Affairs, DOC, Pardons and Paroles, DHR, Red Cross, local EMA, and the Walker County government.

By the end of the first day of recovery operations, 87 bodies had been located. Within 24 hours of the initial discovery, GEMA had set up a toll-free Family Information Line for family members to call. GEMA assimilated grief counselors and facilitated a meeting with local funeral homes to coordinate assistance in body identification.

The recovery effort cost was some $9 million. Due to the unprecedented nature of the incident, Gov. Barnes submitted a letter to President George W. Bush requesting that it be declared a Presidential Disaster, but we were denied. In a letter from Federal Emergency Management

Agency (FEMA) Director Joe Allbaugh, we were not only turned down for the aid, but were told we should have been ashamed and embarrassed to even ask for the help.

Among the expenses we had included spending $1,500 for diesel fuel every 24 hours just to keep the generators running to keep things cool in the makeshift morgue. We had the DMORT (Disaster Mortuary Operational Response Team) running the body identification portion of the operation for us. They respond to large scale disasters all over the U.S. to help with the identification process of the deceased individuals, as well as storage of the bodies until they are claimed or reburied. They didn't bill us for their services since we weren't given federal aid. That alone was a tremendous savings to the state.

Ray Brent Marsh was arrested and charged with more than 300 criminal violations. He eventually pleaded guilty and was sentenced to 12 years in prison. Marsh received credit for the time he had spent in custody and was released from Central State Prison in Bibb County (GA) on June 29, 2016.

We started off using volunteers to help in the recovery effort, but that didn't work so we ended up using all state folks. We also brought in state personnel to work with the families who began calling about their loved ones. Members of the probation department were among the workers so that put Diane in the middle of the activity rather

It's All About The People

Ray Brent Marsh being arrested at the Tri-State Crematory.

than just hearing about it from me when I came home at night.

Here's her thoughts on the tragedy:

I cried a lot, so did a lot of other people helping the families. For example, a woman called about her son. She said, "Did y'all find a little boy about 8 years old in his baseball outfit?" I said, "Ma'am I don't know but I'll certainly try to find out for you." She said, "He wanted to be buried in his baseball outfit. He even had his cap on."

She went on to tell me what color tennis shoes he had on and all types of things about him. She said, "Do you think they'll be able to tell it's him?" I didn't know if they would, so I just let her talk it out. That really, really got to me.

I had a few of them say things like, "Well, my baby may be down there. Did y'all find a baby about four or five days old? I lost him right after birth."

It was tough, but it wasn't as tough on us as it was on the others who had to go down there (to the crematory) and see the bodies. Some of the officers who were down there helping with the body recovery effort had to see counselors. They were having such a hard time dealing with what they were seeing.

Inside one of the tents set up to house the workers as they recover the remains.

It's All About The People

Before I went up there, I felt bad for the families, but I was thinking it would be older people we were asking about. But when you start talking to these families and they are talking about babies and 8-year-olds and what they were wearing, it got personal. I don't know if they found the little boy in the baseball outfit or not. We just gathered information and turned it in for the workers to use. When I think about that little boy now, it's just like it was yesterday that I talked to the mother. It had that much of an effect on me.

It was rough on everyone. Georgia Senator Max Cleland (a disabled US Army veteran of the Vietnam War), came up to observe the situation. He and I, along with some other people, were on one of the Gator all-terrain vehicles going around the area. He looked at me and said, "Director, get

The discovery at the Tri-State Crematory drew national and international media attention.

me out of here. This reminds me too much of what I saw in Vietnam."

When I initially walked up to the scene, you could see bodies lying around in the backyard. There was an old pole barn with tin siding on it behind the house and that was where some of the bodies were. It was there that I saw bodies of people I knew. You look at it and say, "Is this real?" You look around and then you see some folks you actually recognize, and you wonder how is this possible? I knew the senior Marshes quite well. They had been in the crematory business about the whole time I'd been sheriff. In fact, the Tri-State Crematory was one of the first such facilities established in Georgia.

There was a hole in the backyard of Marsh Jr.'s residence where he had put bodies. You could tell he got more cynical as time went on, even with

The command center where workers assisted family members who had loved ones on the site.

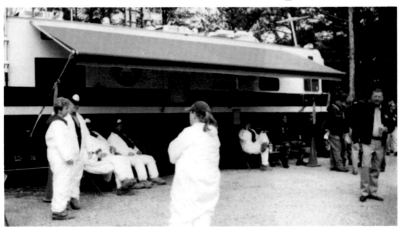

Workers taking a break at the Tri-State Crematory.

the hole containing the bodies we unearthed. When they first started (putting bodies in the hole), they were kind of placed in there. The last hole we found, looked like you had back up to the hole with wood in your truck and just dumped it in there.

It was a total disregard for human life or human dignity. Being raised on a farm, we were taught to cover up cattle when we buried them, not just throw them in a hole and drive off. Thinking about the baseball youth, I just don't see how you could lay down at night and go to sleep.

Those families had already gone through the grief process of losing their loved one. Then they had to go through the grief process of finding out if their loved one was lying up there on the ground and the ashes they had was only cement dust and/ or horse manure. A lot of people brought their urns and the GBI tested the contents to determine

what it really was. <u>Very few</u> of the human remains were found in them.

To me, when the caskets came out of the ground (in South Georgia during the 1994 flood), was pretty tough. They were scattered about, but you couldn't get mad at anyone - this event was a natural disaster. At the crematory you had someone you could get mad at and criticize. There was a lot of hard work up there.

To make sure we had done a complete job, we cut all the timber on the property and drained a small three-acre lake on the property. Draining the lake was a process in itself, as that lake drained into the City of LaFayette drinking water reservoir. That operation had to be managed carefully. The lake was pumped out instead of the dam being cut. We took an irrigation pump and pumped the lake dry with a six inch pipe with filters in it to make sure nothing got into the City of LaFayette's drinking water. No bodies were found in the lake bed.

We got the Interior Department to bring in their four-wheelers that had x-ray machines attached. They x-rayed the ground, then we cut three feet of dirt off and they x-rayed it again to be sure that we had made every effort to locate any bodies that might have been there. Once they said there were no more bodies there, then that was as confident as we could be.

We discovered 339 sets of remains dating

back to 1997 and 222 of those were identified. Bodies were returned to family members. Those bodies not claimed were properly buried in a cemetery near the Georgia/Tennessee line with markers so that if a family member came forward at a later date, the remains could be located.

The recovery operation took six weeks as it covered a 16-acre site. More than 500 First Responders were initially involved in the operation. Following the incident at the Tri-State Crematory, legislation was introduced in Georgia to strengthen state regulations for crematoriums and to make the abuse of dead bodies a felony. It's my understanding that the situation also resulted in actions in other states and even on the national level.

Another look inside one of the tents set up to house the workers as they recover the remains.

An aerial view of the Tri-State Crematory as the recovery process was going on.

The remains that were recovered from the property of the Tri-State Crematory in the Noble Community of Walker County, GA.

It's All About The People
Scenes from Tri-State Crematory

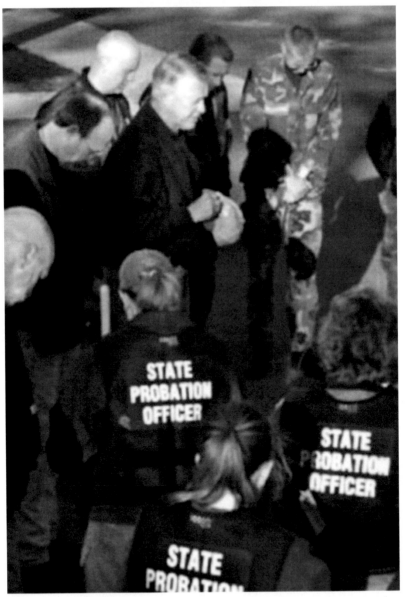

Workers and volunteers take a moment for prayer and reflection while working the scene at the Tri-State Crematory.

Gary W. McConnell

A tent set up for the workers to gather items needed to recover the remains discovered on the Marsh property.

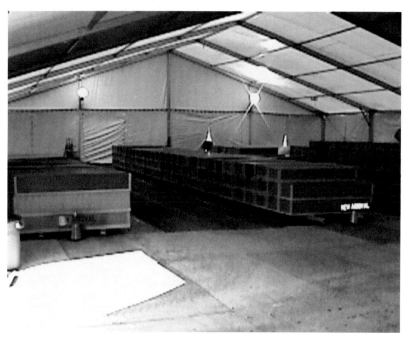

The makeshift morgue set up in a tent where the recovered remains were properly cared for until they could be returned to family members or buried.

335

It's All About The People

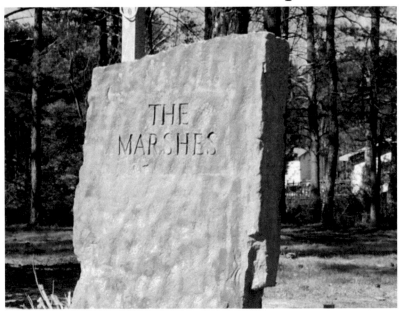

The sign the Marsh Family had erected leading into their property in the Noble Community north of LaFayette, GA.

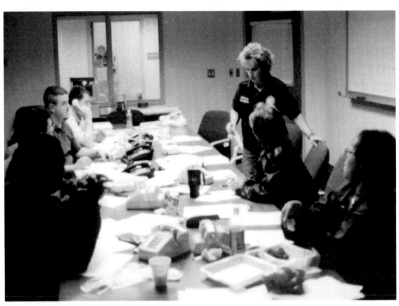

Call center in Walker County for the Tri-State Crematory and Marsh Operation to receive family member calls and to contact the family members.

336

24
Another Change

After serving one term (four years), Roy Barnes lost the governor's race to Sonny Perdue who became governor of Georgia in 2003.

I worked with Gov. Perdue from January to March (2003) and had a good working relationship with him. He had asked me after the tornado in Pickens County (which happened just prior to his taking office) to give him a proposal on how GEMA and Homeland Security should be run. I also brought in several federal folks from the Department of Justice to meet with him during the transition time. All indications were that I was going to continue on in my role (as GEMA Director). In fact, that was what was said.

After he took offce, Gov. Perdue asked all agency heads for their resignation. We all gave him one. It's not out of the ordinary, especially when an administration changes parties, to ask agency heads for resignations. This was a new party and the first time they had been in control of the governor's office in some 150 years.

After I submitted my resignation, I was basically told to continue what I was doing, that I was doing a good job, not to worry about it. We

continued operating at GEMA like we had been doing.

I was on my way to lunch around 11:30 a.m. on March 18 when I got a call from a gentleman named Bill Hitchens. He had been appointed head of the Georgia State Patrol by Gov. Perdue. Bill told me the Govenor had decided to accept my resignation. I told him, "Bill, I haven't resigned again. I resigned one time and he (the Governor) told me to stay. I haven't resigned. Maybe he's going to fire me, but I haven't resigned again." Bill said, "Well, he wants you out of the office by 5 o'clock."

In May of 2003 I arranged for Lt. Governor Mark Taylor to participate in the Railroad Turntable Dedication held by the City of Summerville. On hand for the ribbon cutting was (left to right) Rep. Barbara Massey Reece, Summerville Mayor Joe R. Norton, myself, Lt. Gov. Taylor, and Senator Preston Smith.

I turned around, went back to my office and got my things. This was at 11:30 in the morning, ironically the Govenor was holding a press conference at noon that same day naming someone else as the director of GEMA.

He had every right to fire me. I do not question that at all because it (being Director of GEMA) was a political job and I respect that. As I said then and I still say today, I just didn't like the way he did it.

25
Honored by
The House

In 2003, shortly after leaving GEMA, I was honored by the Georgia House of Representatives for my 12 years of service to the state as director of GEMA.

The House passed a resolution presented by Reps. Barbara Massey Reece, D-Menlo, and Mike Snow, D-Chickamauga, along with Reps. Jenkins of the 93rd district, Coleman of the 118th,

On hand for the House of Representatives resolution honoring me were (left to right) Dade County Sheriff Phillip Street, Rep. Mike Snow from Walker County, Chattooga County Sheriff Ralph Kellett, myself, Rep. Barbara Massey Reece from Chattooga County, and Bill Blackwell, who had worked with me in GEMA.

sand Boggs of the 145th district. The resolution noted my "reputation for excellence as the state coordinator of emergency response efforts."

It was a great honor for me and my family. It was also an honor for the public safety community.

In recognition of the honor, Rep. Reece said, "Chattooga County residents are proud of Mr. McConnell. In Chattooga County and all across the state, Gary McConnell has great respect and a flawless reputation. He never asked anyone serving under him to do anything he wouldn't do or wasn't doing already."

Others on hand for the resolution on the House floor were (left to right) Terry Norris, executive director of the Georgia Sheriff's Association; Monroe County Sheriff John Cary Bittick, president of the National Sheriff's Association; Dade County Sheriff Phillip Street; Becky, our daughter; myself; Diane; Chattooga County Sheriff Ralph Kellett; and Whitfield County Sheriff Scott Chitwood.

It's All About The People

Rep. Snow had this to say, "Mr. McConnell is deserving of recognition for the way he responded to all state emergency operations. Gary McConnell is a gentle man of great stature, great character, and great integrity. Gary McConnell is a friend to all of us in Northwest Georgia."

Gary W. McConnell

House Resolution 756
By: Representatives Snow of the 1st, Reece of the 11th, Jenkins of the 93rd, Coleman of the
118th, and Boggs of the 145th

A RESOLUTION

1 Commending Gary W. McConnell; and for other purposes.

2 WHEREAS, Gary W. McConnell has served with the utmost ability as Director of the
3 Georgia Emergency Management Agency (GEMA) since January, 1991, and has earned a
4 reputation for excellence as the state coordinator of emergency response efforts; and

5 WHEREAS, he began his career in law enforcement in 1965 as a deputy to his father, Sheriff
6 John Frank McConnell of Chattooga County, and following his sudden death Gary served
7 as the sheriff for more than two decades and was past president of the Georgia Sheriff's
8 Association before he was appointed to GEMA; and

9 WHEREAS, under his leadership, Georgia created a Severe Storms Research Center,
10 expanded the National Oceanic and Atmospheric Administration (NOAA) Weather Radio
11 network throughout the state, acquired a mobile communications vehicle, and established
12 training and standards for the 911 service and for private search and rescue dog teams; and

13 WHEREAS, he was Chief of Staff for the State Olympic Law Enforcement Command and
14 coordinated 29 state agencies for the 1996 Summer Olympics, was cochairman of the
15 National Emergency Management Association's Terrorism Committee, a member of
16 Georgia's Homeland Security Task Force, and his dedicated public service has been highly
17 valued.

18 NOW, THEREFORE, BE IT RESOLVED BY THE HOUSE OF REPRESENTATIVES that
19 the members of this body recognize and commend Gary W. McConnell for his diligence and
20 leadership as the Director of the Georgia Emergency Management Agency (GEMA) and
21 convey to him their sincere appreciation of his outstanding public service and best wishes.

22 BE IT FURTHER RESOLVED that the Clerk of the House of Representatives is authorized
23 and directed to transmit an appropriate copy of this resolution to Gary W. McConnell.

H. R. 756
- 1 -

343

26
After GEMA

My desire to serve the public continued after I left GEMA. I began working with The Stimson Center located in Wahington, D.C., a nonpartisan policy research center working to protect people, preserve the planet, and promote security and prosperity.

The Stimson Center's award-winning research serves as a roadmap to address borderless threats through concerted action. I worked with them six months. A lot of that time I was mentoring some of the younger people working for them. I also worked with Ms. Amy Smithson, PhD, who is a world-class expert on nuclear weapons and terrorism.

Dr. Smithson specializes in field research on issues related to chemical and biological weapons nonproliferation. Her publications and expertise have drawn invitations to testify before Congress, speak in other venues, and assist the media. She arranged for A.D. Vickery, Deputy Chief, Seattle Fire Department; Leslee Stein Spencer, RN, MS and Director of EMS Services for Illinois; and me to go to Erice, Sicily (Italy) to make a presentation to the World Federation of Scientists (WFS).

The World Federation of Scientists was

founded in Erice, Sicily, in 1973, by a group of imminent scientists led by Isidor Isaac Rabi and Antonino Zichichi. WFS identified 15 classes of Planetary Emergencies and began to organize the fight against these threats. WFS held a series of International Seminars on Nuclear War which have had a tremendous impact on reducing the danger of a planet-wide nuclear disaster and have ultimately contributed to the end of the Cold War.

I attended the 31st Session of the International Seminars on Planetary Emergencies where I was a guest speaker. The focus was on the Cultural Planetary Emergency Case Study: Terrorism. We

Speaking before the World Federation of Scientists in Sicily, Italy, (above) was fascinating and enlightening.

discussed the multidisciplinary global approach and the cross-disciplinary solutions.

Delegates were there to define the contributions of multidisciplinary research and cross-cultural co-operation, which are necessary to reduce the threat of global terrorism to people and to the environment.

My presentation was, "People: The Key Element in Disaster Response." I talked about how police officers, doctors, search and rescue personnel, fire fighters, and a variety of other

I attended the World Federation of Scientists with A.D. Vickery, Deputy Chief, Seattle Fire Department; and Leslee Stein Spencer, RN, MS and Director of EMS Services for Illinois.

public servants are the most critical asset in any emergency response.

I used two cases to illustrate a series of points about the importance of people in the emergency response equation, as well as various law enforcement and emergency management challenges that occur during major events.

The cases I talked about were the 1996 summer Olympic Games and the January 1997 bombing of a family planning clinic, both in Atlanta. I concluded with a series of recommendations about how to improve disaster response.

Attending one of the presentations at the World Federation of Scientists with Leslee Stein Spencer and A.D. Vickery in Erice, Sicily.

It's All About The People

It was a learning experience not only concerning terrorism, but in getting to know more about the people, culture and area. Diane was able to go with me and we had time to visit some of the surrounding communities and businesses.

Gary W. McConnell

A street scene from Sicily, Italy, where I made a presentation to the World Federation of Scientists while working for The Stimson Center.

This castle (above) is on the island of Sicily where I made my presentation in the little mountain town of Erice, Italy.

Working with The Stimson Center was always meant to be only a short-term partnership. While there, I had been talking with Innovative Emergency Management (IEM) about a consulting position.

IEM is a North Carolina headquartered risk management company founded in 1985 by CEO Madhu Beriwal. IEM has eight offices strategically located around the United States.

Their areas of specialty include homeland security and emergency management, information technology, defense support, and program integration support. IEM works with government agencies and private sector organizations around the world to improve disaster preparedness, response, recovery and strengthen homeland defense, counterterrorism, and public agency performance.

At IEM, we build scientific tools and develop data-driven strategies that help our customers achieve measurable results — saving lives, reducing costs, increasing efficiencies, and improving decision making.

Shortly after Hurricane Katrina hit the Gulf

Coast, numerous children were missing. IEM was headquartered in Baton Rouge, LA., at that time and we were doing work related to Hurricane Katrina. Madhu Beriwal is the owner of IEM and she wanted to do something to help find those children.

I arranged for Madhu to make a presentation

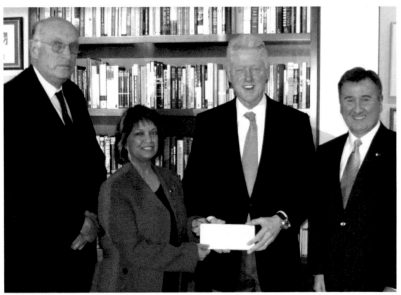

IEM CEO Madhu Beriwal (above) believes in helping others not only by teaching through her company, but also financially. She is presenting a $100,000 check to former President Bill Clinton for the Bush-Clinton Katrina Fund. The fund was created following the aftermath of Hurricane Katrina and the devastation it caused. The fund provided relief and rebuilding resources to help the hurricane victims. On hand for the presentation, was myself and Wayne Thomas, senior vice president of Homeland Security and Emergency Management for IEM. On the same day, we presented another $100,000 check from IEM to John Walsh for the National Center for Missing and Exploited Children.

to the Bush-Clinton Katrina Fund. We went to New York where she presented former President Bill Clinton with a $100,000 check for the fund. The presentation was made in President Clinton's office overlooking Central Park. On the same day we presented a check for an equal amount to John Walsh for the National Center for Missing and Exploited Children fund.

At IEM, I worked with Wayne Thomas, senior vice president of Homeland Security and Emergency Management for the company. Upon his leaving the company in 2016, he sent me a letter noting some of the accompishments and the significant impact on improving preparedness in the U.S. we had achieved working together.

Some of the items included:

* Performing the Department of Homeland Security National Intelligence Center technical assistance program to provide technical assistance to hundreds of states, regions, and local communities.

*Piloting and expanding FEMA's catastrophic planning program, beginning with the Hurricane Pam project in southeastern Louisiana and the eight-state New Madrid catastrophic earthquake planning project.

* Working with the governments of every U.S. state on the planning, design, and execution of programs related to some of the most dangerous hazards the world has faced, including chemical

weapons and terrorism incidents, nuclear/ radiological incidents, public health emergencies, and natural disasters.

* Provided leadership for the presidentially mandated Nationwide Plan Review, guiding reviews of emergency plans in 65 U.S. jurisdictions, as well as staffing and managing federal operations centers that responded to terrorism incidents and natural disasters, including Hurricanes Katrina and Rita.

We met with senior leadership at federal and state agencies related to all major natural and man-made incidents in the U.S. We also worked directly with several Governors and attended numerous National Governor Association meetings.

Wayne said, "With your support, we have been able to build greater visibility for IEM and significantly expand the company's work in the homeland security and emergency management markets. Our record of accomplishments for the past 13 years provides the foundation for IEM's future growth in Homeland Security and Emergency Management."

At IEM, I provided expert assistance and facilitation support for FEMA's catastrophic planning and delivered technical assistance to state and local jurisdictions across the U.S. under an IEM contract with FEMA's National Preparedness Directorate, Capabilities Division.

Wayne and I became close personal friends

over the years that we worked together. When he met and married his wife, Ishleen, the ceremony took place at our house. It was truly an international event. She was from India, he was from Wales and it was performed in Teloga, Georgia. We were very honored!

In 2017 I left my retainer position with IEM, but continued to work with them as a consultant as needed. Now it's on a case by case basis.

It's All About The People

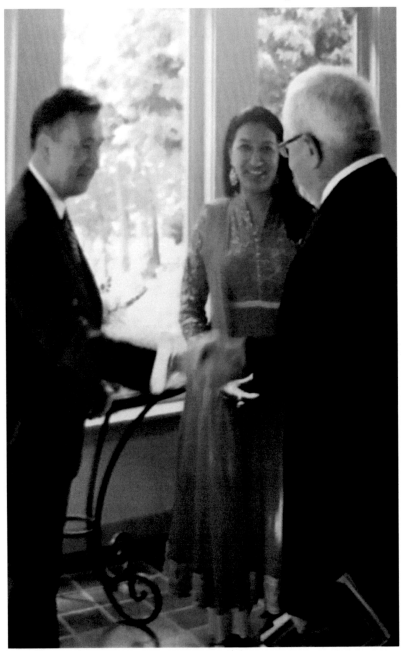

Wayne and Ishleen Thomas on their wedding day at our house on May 2, 2014 with Chattooga County Probate Judge Jon Payne (right) who officiated at their ceremony.

28
Career Recap

A short time after I left GEMA and began working as a security consultant I was interviewed by Stump Martin, a staff writer with the Chattanooga Times Free Press out of Chattanooga, TN.

The interview was about my career and the paths I had followed throughout the years. It also included my thoughts and concerns for and about the people of Georgia and the United States going forward. Below is that interview entitled, "Security is long-standing concern of Gary McConnell." It has been reprinted here in its entirety with the permission of the Chattanooga Times Free Press.

SUMMERVILLE, Ga. - Gary McConnell got his start in politics as the youngest sheriff in Georgia history when he was appointed to replace his father, who died in office in 1965.

Two years later, at age 21, he became the youngest man in Georgia history elected sheriff.

Mr. McConnell climbed the public safety ladder and served as Georgia Emergency Management Agency director for 12 years after being appointed by Gov. Zell Miller in January

1991. On March 18, 2003, Gov. Sonny Perdue appointed Mike Sherberger to replace him at GEMA.

The move came a day after the federal Department of Homeland Security raised the national threat level from "elevated" to "high risk" for terrorist attack, or level orange.

During his tenure as the GEMA director, Mr. McConnell doled out more than $1 billion in relief aid. He served as chief of staff for the State Olympic Law Enforcement Command during the 1996 Centennial Olympic Games in Atlanta, coordinating 29 agencies and nearly 5,000 law enforcement officers.

Mr. McConnell was Terrorism Committee chairman at the time he left his GEMA post.

National Emergency Management Agency Executive Director Trina Hembree Sheets said, "There are not a lot of people in this country with his expertise and experience in the field of terrorism."

She said he has testified before congressional hearings on terrorism and has the respect of every emergency management director in the country.

Mr. McConnell is working as a security consultant and has just returned from viewing the damage in Alabama, Mississippi and Louisiana caused by Hurricane Katrina.

Mr. McConnell answered questions last

week for the Chattanooga Times Free Press.

Q. After serving as the chief of staff for the State Olympic Law Enforcement Command during the 1996 Olympic Games in Atlanta, what is your reaction to the Eric Rudolph sentence for the Olympic Park bombing?

A: I'm pleased he was caught and by local law enforcement. There was a tremendous amount of money spent and a lot of man-hours in catching him. I'm glad he is now in custody.

What he did was devastating to the community. Not only did Eric Rudolph kill and injure people, but hundreds of people could have died or been injured. I'm sure the judge made a decision he thought was fair. But personally, I think he should have gotten the electric chair.

Q: How we handle and prepare for terrorist disasters changed after 9/11. How will the destruction and devastation of Hurricane Katrina change the way we prepare for natural disasters?

A: Most focus after 9/11 was on buying equipment. Regardless of the cause of the event, 60-75 percent requires response from the same people. The difference between terrorism and natural disasters is law enforcement plays a much larger role in terrorism.

But, others are playing the same role

dealing with evacuation, sheltering, rebuilding the community, dealing with victims, body identification and family notification.

Now we need to integrate it all into a seamless response and recovery. Nine-eleven changed the way we prepared for disasters, not only through Homeland Security, but the amount of money spent.

It also broadened the perspective of public safety by bringing the Department of Public Health, Department of Agriculture, Public Works and others. Not only did we focus on foreign terrorism, but on home-grown terrorism and natural events in America.

We have to make better use of resources. Hopefully, the Katrina event will help us better integrate the response capabilities.

Q: As the GEMA director you dealt with the South Georgia floods of 1994, Hurricane Opal and the evacuation of more than 350,000 coastal residents for Hurricane Floyd. What advice do you give Mississippi and Louisiana officials on how to build back?

A: Based on my experience with the 1994 floods in 55 counties in Georgia, it will take the area of devastation 12-15 years to build back.

It took eight years to recover in Georgia, and the Katrina damage is 10 times worse. In short

and long term, recovery officials must look at the big picture. They need to think of where they're going to rebuild. Are they going to rebuild in a flood plain? If so, they need to look at what we did in Chickamauga where we raised the houses.

They don't need to jump in too quickly trying to solve the immediate need. For example, does it make sense in Mississippi for the casinos to be built back on the water?

This was a life-changing event for thousands of people. Remember, disasters are about people and not stuff. They need to be considerate of the individuals. Some actions might create more problems.

Q: Do you believe Georgia is prepared in case of a similar disaster?

A: We had 17 presidential disasters when I was the GEMA director, and we got better with each one by learning from our mistakes. To me, the floods of 1994 were the state's most trying time, but also its finest hour.

The 1996 Olympic Games spotlighted Georgia in a positive manner. We had dedicated leadership from the governor's office on down. A tremendous amount of credit goes to the city and county personnel around the state. But, I think we have lost some of that in Georgia because of a void in the state leadership. The state needs to be in tune with the needs of the community, and we have lost some of that across the state.

It's All About The People

It takes experienced leadership and the ability to work well with others to gain the trust of the people you are working with. We're missing that trust and vision on the state level.

Q: In your professional opinion, are there terrorist networks operating in the United States? If so, how should they be dealt with?

A: I believe there are at least some sleeper cells in the United States. But, it is important that we don't just worry about al-Qaida cells and forget the home-grown terror.

Terrorism is like beauty: It's all in the eyes of the beholder. It doesn't have to be in Atlanta's Centennial Park or in New York City or Oklahoma City. It can be local when a person walks into a school with an AK-47. If we can't respond to the small events, we can't deal with the big events.

What we can't let happen is to trample our constitutional rights to fight terror. If we change our constitutional rights, the terrorists have won. Their purpose is to change our lives through pain, death and fear.

Q: Is the Homeland Security plan working?

A: It needs to be evaluated and improved upon. If there's an event and we don't improve on how to handle them, then the people don't need to be in those positions to make the decisions.

29
Awards & Plaques

I have been honored throughout my career to have received numerous awards, plaques and recognition from various individuals, organizations, groups, and municipalities.

The following pages are just a few of those wonderful acknowledgements that are dear to my heart and a delightful reminder of my time helping others.

An award from the Israel Police for their time working with GEMA and me during the 1996 Olympics. Their second in command spent a great deal of time in Atlanta prior and during the Olympics as an advisor on security issues. We learned a lot from them and they were very instrumental in the success of the 1996 games in Georgia.

364

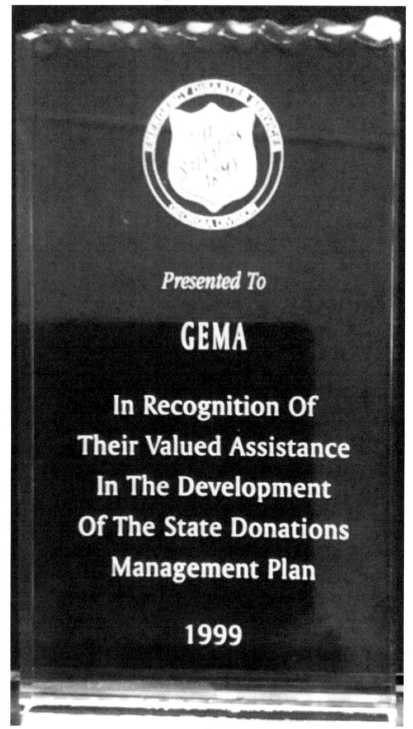

Presented To

GEMA

In Recognition Of
Their Valued Assistance
In The Development
Of The State Donations
Management Plan

1999

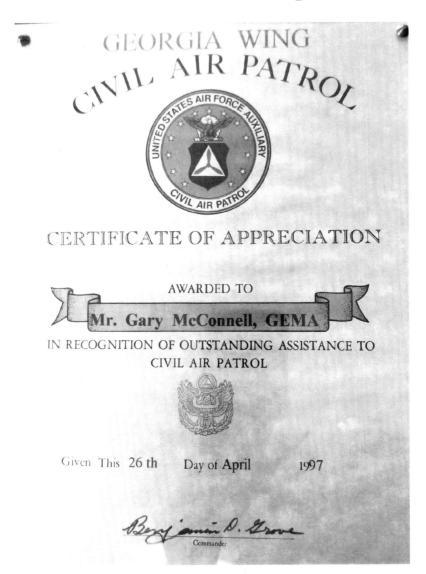

GEORGIA WING

CIVIL AIR PATROL

CERTIFICATE OF APPRECIATION

AWARDED TO

Mr. Gary McConnell, GEMA

IN RECOGNITION OF OUTSTANDING ASSISTANCE TO
CIVIL AIR PATROL

Given This 26 th Day of April 1997

Benjamin D. Grove
Commander

*Back in late 1996 and 1997 technology wasn't anything
like it is now. During that time, we at GEMA worked with
the Civil Air Patrol where they could fly a disaster scene
and live video it back to the State Operations Center. It
was cutting edge technology at that time.*

The 1994 Flood completely destroyed the Macon Water Treatment Plant. GEMA rebuilt it and the groundbreaking ceremonies were held in November 1996. The shovel award was given to me in recognition of that effort.

SPECIAL AWARD OF
RECOGNITION

Presented to the

Georgia Emergency
Management Agency

In Appreciation for Assistance
to Counties Impacted during the
FLOOD OF 1994

By the

ASSOCIATION
COUNTY COMMISSIONERS
OF GEORGIA

October, 1994

Federal Emergency
Management Agency

CERTIFICATE OF APPRECIATION

Gary McConnell
and the staff of the
Georgia Emergency Management Agency

For the leadership and the intiative shown in creating
outstanding public education products to protect the
public from the risk of hurricanes.

James L. Witt
James L. Witt
Director

March 9, 1994

FF 76-19, AUG 90

30
ABOUT THE AUTHOR

Gary W. McConnell was born in Summerville, GA, in December of 1944, the only child of John Frank and Marguerite (Rea) McConnell.

He attended the two-room school house in the Teloga Community near his home until the school closed and then he completed the sixth through

Sheriff Gary W. McConnell

It's All About The People

the eighth grade at the Menlo Elementary School.

He was a member of the first graduating class from the Chattooga High School in Summerville in 1962. He attended Mississippi State University, but had to leave abruptly due to his father's illness.

Growing up on a farm in Chattooga County, Gary learned the values of determination, hard work and commitment to public service from his

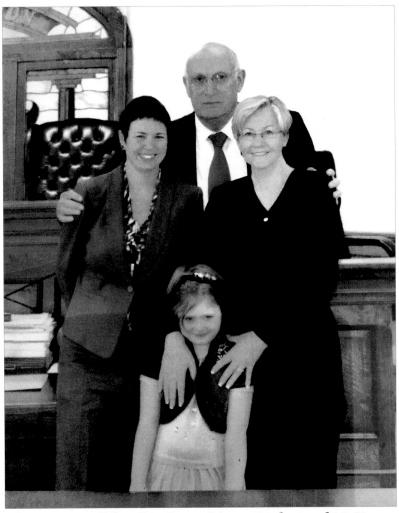

The McConnell family: Gary, Diane, Becky, and McKenna

mother, who worked as a rural mail carrier, and by his father's failures and successes as a farmer, businessman, and county sheriff.

Following in his dad's footsteps, Gary began his career in law enforcement as a sheriff's deputy in Chattooga County actually working for his dad. After the untimely death of his father, Gary was appointed sheriff by the probate judge and in a special election made history as Georgia's youngest elected sheriff.

He proudly served as sheriff of Chattooga County for more than two decades before going on

Following in the McConnell tradition of serving the public, Becky McConnell (right) takes the oath as a new attorney in the Georgia Bar Association. Swearing in the new attorney is Superior Court Judge Kristina Cook Graham.

to serve the public on the state level as the director of the Georgia Emergency Management (GEMA) Agency. He then served as Director of SOLEC during the Atlanta Olympic Games in 1996.

After leaving GEMA, Gary continued to serve the people through his association with The Stimson Center, a nonpartisan policy research center, and then with IEM as the Senior Homeland Security and Emergency Management Consultant.

Following in the footsteps of her family, the McConnell's daughter, Becky, graduated from law school, passed the Georgia Bar Exam and became a general practice lawyer. She still continues the McConnell tradition of serving the people.

Gary and his wife, Diane, life-long residents of Northwest Georgia, continue to reside and work in the county they love.

Gary W. McConnell

Gary and Diane McConnell

It's All About The People

Beginning with his humble upbringing in rural northwest Georgia, Gary McConnell has dedicated his life to serving others. Throughout his career beginning as a deputy sheriff, to his over 20 years as the elected sheriff of Chattooga County and later with his appointment as Director of the Georgia Emergency Management Agency, Gary has achieved a high level experience uncommon to most throughout the country. From petty crime and homicide to domestic terrorism and natural disasters, Gary McConnell has a lifetime of unique experience which he graciously shares as he authors this book. We are grateful for the honorable service of our native born son. ... J. Terry Norris, Executive Director, Georgia Sheriffs' Association, Georgia Sheriffs' Youth Homes

* * * * *

"Gary McConnell, a wonderful friend who has served me and Georgia so well." ... Zell Miller, 79th Governor of Georgia

* * * * *

"There are not a lot of people in this country with his expertise and experience in the field of terrorism. He has testified before congressional hearings on terrorism and has the respect of every emergency management director in the country." ... Trina Hembree Sheets, National Emergency Management Agency Executive Director *(reprinted by permission of the Chattanooga Times Free Press)*

* * * * *

"Gary, thanks for all you do for me. Thanks for your friendship. Best wishes." ... Roy E. Barnes, 80th Governor of Georgia